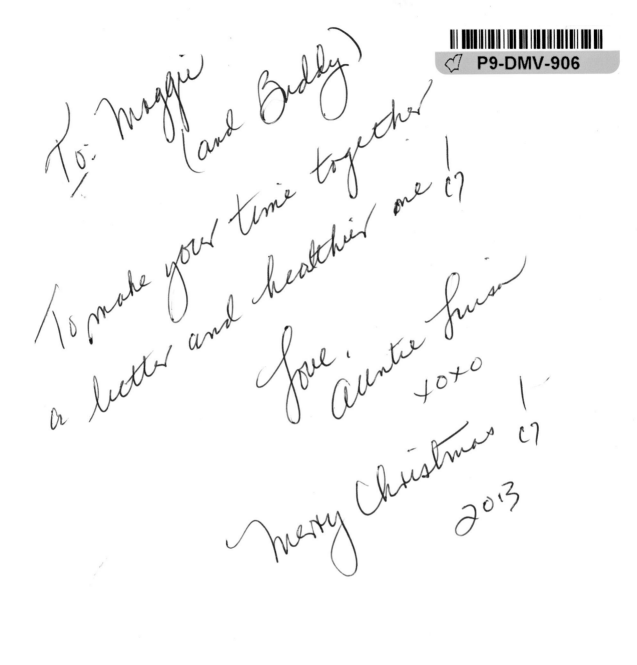

To: Maggie (and Buddy)

To make your time together a better and healthier one! ♡

Love,
Auntie Susan
xoxo

Merry Christmas! ♡
2013

COMPLETE
DOG CARE

COMPLETE
DOG CARE

DK

DK

LONDON, NEW YORK, MELBOURNE,
MUNICH, AND DELHI

DORLING KINDERSLEY
Senior Editor Paula Regan
Project Art Editor Amy Orsborne
Editorial Assistant Alexandra Beeden
Editor Ann Baggaley
US Senior Editor Rebecca Warren
US Editor Kate Johnsen
Jacket Designer Silke Spingies
Jacket Editor Manisha Majithia
Jacket Design Development Manager Sophia Tampakopoulos
Producer, Pre-Production Rebekah Parsons-King
Producer Gemma Sharpe
Photographer Gary Ombler
Managing Art Editor Karen Self
Publisher Laura Buller
Art Director Phil Ormerod
Associate Publishing Director Liz Wheeler
Publishing Director Jonathan Metcalf

Consultant Editor Kim Dennis-Bryan
Contributors Adam Beral, Katie John, Alison Logan

DK INDIA
Senior Art Editor Anis Sayyed
Art Editor Neha Wahi
Assistant Art Editors Astha Singh, Radhika Kapoor
Managing Art Editor Arunesh Talapatra
Senior Editor Sreshtha Bhattacharya
Editor Antara Moitra
Assistant Editor Archana Ramachandran
Managing Editor Pakshalika Jayaprakash
Picture Research Surya Sarangi
Senior DTP Designer Jagtar Singh
DTP Designers Bimlesh Tiwary, Rajesh Singh Adhikari, Arjinder Singh
DTP Manager/CTS Balwant Singh
Production Manager Pankaj Sharma

First American Edition, 2013
Published in the United States by
DK Publishing
375 Hudson Street
New York, New York 10014

13 14 15 16 10 9 8 7 6 5 4 3 2 1
001 – 184790 – Apr/13

Published in Great Britain
by Dorling Kindersley Limited.

A catalog record for this book is available from the Library of Congress.

ISBN 978-1-4654-0221-9

DK books are available at special discounts when purchased in bulk for sales promotions,
premiums, fund-raising, or educational use. For details contact: DK Publishing Special
Markets, 375 Hudson Street, New York, New York 10014 or SpecialSales@dk.com

Printed and bound in China by Leo Paper Products Ltd.

Discover more at
www.dk.com

Disclaimer

Every effort has been made to ensure that the information in this book is accurate.
Neither the publishers or the authors accept any legal responsibility for any personal
injury or injuries to dogs or other damage or loss arising from the undertaking of any
of the activities or exercises presented in this book, or from the reliance on any advice
in this book. If your dog is ill or has behavioral problems, please seek the advice of
a qualified professional, such as a vet or behavioral expert.

Contents

▽ **Grooming needs**
Whether you have a short-haired, long-haired, or curly-haired dog, all breeds need grooming regularly to keep them looking and feeling their best.

△ **Friend for life**
Choosing a new puppy or adult dog to join your family is an exciting experience, but one that comes with big responsibilities.

▽ **Grooming needs**
Whether you have a short-haired, long-haired, or curly-haired dog, all breeds need grooming regularly to keep them looking and feeling their best.

△ **Out and about**
Regular exercise is vital for your dog's mental and physical health. Whether "free running," walking on a lead, or playing games of fetch, it is a time you can enjoy together.

Introduction

The connection between an owner and dog can be a deeply rewarding relationship. Dogs have coexisted with humans for thousands of years, and today they still fulfill many important jobs—not least as loyal companions and much-loved members of our households. Dogs are dependent on us for all their needs, and as dog owners it is our job to keep our animals physically healthy and to give them the opportunity to express their natural instincts. This book will

introduce you to all aspects of essential dog care, from carrying out regular health checks to setting basic rules for training, so that you can build a happy and healthy life with your dog.

Bringing a new dog into your life requires preparation and planning. If you don't yet own a dog, this book offers guidance on choosing a puppy or adult dog that is right for your household and lifestyle, together with an overview of popular breeds and their specific training, grooming, and exercise needs. There's advice on making your home safe and comfortable for a new dog, and on helping your pet to settle into your household including getting him used to new people and other pets, and tips on how to care for him while traveling or if you go away.

All dogs, whatever their size, age, or breed, require a certain level of daily care and attention in the form of diet, exercise, play, and grooming. Your dog needs a healthy, balanced diet to give him all the nutrients he needs. This book will show you how to tailor a diet suitable for your dog's age and activity level, and details the foods that may be unhealthy or even harmful. Hints and tips on exercise and play, followed by

guidance on grooming and bathing are included to help you give your dog the best possible care.

Basic training is fundamental to a good working relationship between you and your dog—one in which you are a gentle but effective "pack leader." The friendships that we enjoy with other people don't work with dogs. They feel most secure if they can trust us to be a firm but kind "leader." Whether you own a puppy or an older dog, this book has information on positive training methods that your dog will easily understand and accept, as well as ways to structure training

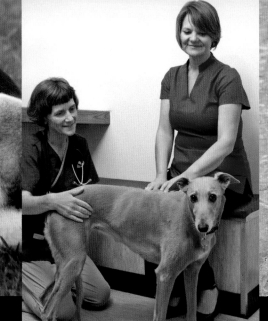

▽ Healthy dog
Make sure your dog always stays in top condition with thorough checkups at home and regular routine visits to the vet.

△ Itchy coat
Fleas and lice are common for even the most well-groomed dog, but they are easily controlled with regular preventive treatments.

△ Extra care
Your dog will need more help and attention in his later years, and there are many ways to make him more comfortable—a few small changes can make a big difference.

sessions. There is step-by-step information on teaching basic commands such as "sit" and "stay," and training your dog to walk on a lead; as well as a look at fun, social activities such as canine sports and agility competitions.

An important part of being a good owner is keeping your dog healthy and dealing promptly with any illnesses or injuries. This book will provide you with a basic understanding of the disorders and diseases that may affect your dog at some point in his life and, most importantly, to help you recognize the warning signs of when to take

him to your vet. A checklist of the signs of good health, and poor health, is included plus advice on routine checks to be done by you or your vet, and top tips on avoiding possible health problems. From serious disorders such as heart disease to minor but irritating ailments like itchy fleas, information is given on all the various health issues that can affect your dog, plus advice on how to care for him while he recuperates.

Injuries and emergencies involving dogs can be frightening for you as well as the dog. This book covers the principles of lifesaving and guides you through the initial steps needed to

▽ **Staying safe**
Minimizing risk when out with your dog is the best way to prevent accidents. Keep your dog on a short lead when walking on the road.

▽ **A new home**
Finding suitable owners and homes for your puppies is one of your most important responsibilities as a breeder.

△ **New additions**
If you decide to breed your dog, make sure you are prepared for the whelping process and the special care that the newborn puppies will need in their early days.

cope with injuries and other serious conditions, as well as giving advice on avoiding dangers such as hypothermia and heat stroke. Having an understanding of basic canine first aid will help you to feel prepared and in control, should you ever find yourself in a situation that requires it.

For a dog owner, the thought of bringing up your own puppies can be irresistible; however, breeding needs to be approached in a very careful, responsible way. Should you decide to go ahead, there is advice on the issues that you need to think about, as well as detailed information on caring for your dog

during pregnancy and whelping (giving birth), and while she is nursing her puppies. This book also has guidance on caring for your puppies in their first weeks, and helping them develop, plus tips on finding loving and secure homes for your youngsters.

Owning a dog is a long-term commitment and comes with a great deal of responsibility, but the rewards for both you and your dog are immense. In this book you will find all the information and advice you need to ensure you will have a well-behaved, happy, and healthy canine companion for many years to come.

1

Your **new dog**

Becoming a dog owner

A dog can be a fantastic, fun addition to your home—but dogs are also complex, intelligent animals and need a lot of care and attention. Owning a dog is a big responsibility.

First considerations

Before buying or adopting a dog, you need to think very carefully about what kind you want and how you plan to look after him. Keep in mind that dogs can live for up to 18 years; you need to be committed to caring for your pet over his entire lifespan.

Do you have other pets or very young children? Is anyone in your home allergic to dogs?

Find out about suitable breeds in advance (pp.20–3). Remember though that temperament is more important than looks. Could you cope with an active dog with lots of energy, or would you prefer a calm

What age is best? A puppy will learn to fit in with your family's routine as he grows up, but at first he will need extra care and should not be left alone for long periods. So if everyone is out of the house all day, you may be better off adopting an adult dog.

Would you prefer a male or a female? Males tend to be more affectionate with people but can be easily distracted during training. Unneutered males can also be aggressive. Females are thought to be calmer with children.

> "Dogs are **not cheap pets** so be sure you can **afford** the **costs of care**. They also **need** a lot of **company**, especially as puppies."

First, you need to be sure that a dog is the right pet for you. Do you have the time to look after, train, and play with a puppy? Can you afford to keep a dog? Is your home environment suitable (pp.24–5)?

one? Do you need a dog who is good with children? Large dogs can require a lot of care and will need more food, which can be expensive, so would you be just as happy with a smaller dog?

△ **Grooming**
All dogs need regular grooming and baths but if you choose a long-haired breed, be aware that you may have to devote a lot of time to these tasks.

◁ **A trial run**
A good way to find out whether life as a dog owner is right for you is by offering to look after a friend's or relative's dog for a few days as a trial run.

▷ **A family pet**
If you have young children, see if you can
introduce them to different breeds or types of
dogs to find out which ones your children prefer.

Essentials of dog care

Dogs are not cheap pets so you
need to be sure you can afford the
costs of care. The likely costs for
your new dog include:
■ Food each day—food is a major
cost, especially for large dogs.
■ Pet insurance—premiums vary
considerably between providers
and depend on the age and breed
of dog and your home location.
■ Accessories such as collar, lead,
food bowls, bed, and medications.
■ Allowance for possible extra
costs such as vet bills or a boarding
kennel if you go away.

Work out how much time per day
you can commit to your dog. When
will you feed him? When can you

▽ **Looking at dog breeds**
Take the chance to watch different breeds
in action at a dog show or even at an
obedience class so you can get an idea
of their nature as well as appearance.

exercise him—or is there someone
else who can do this? All dogs need
exercise and mental stimulation,
and some need at least an hour
of exercise a day (pp.44–7). Dogs
also need a lot of company,
especially as puppies. In addition,
dogs need regular grooming and
baths; long-haired dogs require
extensive grooming and some
breeds of dogs may require visits
to a professional dog groomer.

Owner's responsibilities

■ Providing nutritious food
and fresh water every day.
■ Enabling your dog to express
normal behavior.
■ Meeting his need for company.
■ Protecting him from, and
treating, illness and injury.
■ Fitting your dog with a collar
and tag in case he gets lost.
■ Cleaning up after your dog
and keeping him under control
in public areas.

You are responsible for your pet's
welfare, and in many countries,
there are even laws to ensure that
pet owners care for their animals
properly. Essential duties include
making sure that your dog has a
safe place to live, good food, and
plenty of company (see box, above).
As a dog owner you also need to
make certain that your pet will not
cause harm to himself or to other
people or animals.

Becoming a dog owner

St. Bernard

Miniature
Pinscher

English
Cocker
Spaniel

German
Shepherd

Canadian
Eskimo

Staffordshire
Bull Terrier

Beagle

Choosing a puppy

Puppies are delightful and will grow to fit your family but they require intensive care and training. It is best to acquire a puppy from the person who bred him if possible, and to meet the pup before you take ownership.

Where to get a puppy

If you prefer to select a pure-bred puppy, ask for advice from your area's kennel club, breed societies, or animal welfare groups for advice on good breeders in your area. If you would be happy with a cross-bred dog, you can often adopt puppies from rescue centers or even from people you might know.

It is always best to buy from the person who bred the puppy. It is unwise to buy from advertisements, because you often can't tell where a puppy comes from. Also avoid pet stores, which can be traumatic places for pups, and which may get their puppies from disreputable "puppy mills." Never buy a pup without meeting him first, and never buy on impulse.

Visiting a breeder

Good breeders provide a "family" environment to give their pups the best start in life. Check that the pups live with their mother and avoid any kennels where pups are shown on their own.

Find a breeder who will allow you to spend time with the litter. Check that the puppies are being raised indoors and with plenty of human contact. Watch for any signs that they may not be used to being in a house—for example, being startled by normal domestic noises, such as a phone ringing. Look at the mother (and father if he is present). Are they friendly? Have they been screened for any inherited diseases associated with that breed? Check that the kennels look and smell clean. Is the pups' sleeping area separate from the bathroom area?

The breeder may ask how much experience you have with that breed or with dogs in general, or how you intend to care for the pup. You should also have the chance to ask questions. Will the puppy be wormed and vaccinated? Will the breeder give you advice for the first few weeks after you have bought your pup, or let you return it if

△ **Mother and puppies**
Young pups should live with their mother and siblings. The breeder should let you meet the mother and see the whole litter together.

> **"Never buy a puppy without meeting him first, never buy on impulse, and never because you feel sorry for him!"**

Owner's checklist from breeder

■ Printout of pedigree
■ Breed registration papers
■ Certificate of inoculations
■ Worming history documentation
■ Printed declaration that the pup is healthy and has a good body structure, and that these factors can be verified by your own vet
■ A diet sheet giving food and feeding regime with a sample of the puppy's current food

△ Family decision
Choosing a puppy is an exciting, emotional experience for children. Select a likely candidate before your children meet the pup to ensure a happy outcome.

▷ Rescue pup
Rescue centers occasionally offer puppies who have been abandoned, orphaned, or whose owner has had to give them up. Since the pups have had a difficult start in life, they may need special care.

things don't work out? Don't forget to collect all necessary information from the breeder (see box, left).

Selecting your puppy

A puppy should enjoy meeting you and being handled. A pup that snaps at you could have a dominant personality and be hard to train, while one that hides from you may need a lot of patience to ensure it

does not grow into a nervous adult. Never pick a puppy because you feel sorry for it!

Look out for any signs of ill health, such as runny eyes or nose, diarrhea, a thin or pot-bellied body, dull fur, or scabby patches.

If you have children, visit the puppies yourself first, then take the children once you have made an initial choice.

Big or small
All young puppies are cute and cuddly, and it can be hard to imagine them growing up into adult-size dogs. Take the time to research different dog breeds, and choose one that will suit your home and lifestyle.

Choosing an adult dog

Although puppies are cute and appealing, you may find that an older dog, which does not need as much training, suits your lifestyle better. You can obtain an adult dog from a rescue center or even from someone you know.

Rescue centers

A common way to acquire an adult dog is from a rescue center. Some rescue shelters are run by animal welfare groups and rehome dogs of many sizes and ages. Others specialize in particular dog breeds that have rehoming issues such as greyhounds after the end of their racing career, or dogs with specific care and training needs such as Dobermans and Staffordshire Bull Terriers. Some breed societies run a breed rescue service, and these can be accessed through breed society websites (see p.185 for contact details).

An adult dog will take time to get used to you; however, he may already have been house-trained and socialized. At a rescue center, the dogs' temperaments will have been assessed so you will know if they need a town or country home, are friendly with other pets and children, and whether or not they need to live with a companion. Whether a pure-bred or cross-bred dog, it is wisest to base your selection on temperament more than looks. Spending time at a rescue center may tell you a lot about the dog's predominant traits.

◁ **Rescue dog**
All dogs need a loving home but dogs from rescue centers may need particular care and patience from their owners. Get to know a new dog first before deciding if he suits you.

> "An adult dog will take **time to get used to you** but he may already have **been socialized.**"

Having an assessment

Many of the dogs at rescue centers will have had difficult experiences such as separation from previous owners or even neglect or abuse, so staff will want to be sure that they go to a loving and protective home. You may have to fill in an application form, attend an interview at the center (perhaps with other family members), and have your home inspected by rescue center staff before being allowed to adopt a pet.

In return, you will have the opportunity to ask questions and meet suitable dogs. The dog may already be neutered and microchipped, and may have a veterinary examination before being handed over to you. You may have to pay an adoption fee, which might cover benefits such as a "starter pack" of food, advice on care and behavioral issues, and help with matters such as pet insurance and guidance on the ongoing cost of owning a dog.

◁ **Family interview**
Rescue center staff will want to interview all members of your family and find out about your home and daily life so they can decide which dogs will best match your lifestyle.

Retired greyhounds
Racing greyhounds who are retired or unfit for running often end up in rescue centers but these gentle, graceful dogs can make very good family companions. They love to chase and are fun to play with.

Choosing a dog breed

Whether you already have a favorite breed in mind or are still trying to decide, the information in this section will help you work out which dogs would fit best with your lifestyle and preferences.

Breed groups

There are hundreds of dog breeds in the world and international organizations classify breeds based on their traditional or current uses. Although a dog's character is most strongly formed by its environment and upbringing, looking at breeds by group can give you a general idea of their needs.

■ Working dogs—this group includes guard and herding dogs. They are easy to train but need plenty of physical and mental activity to keep them happy.

■ Spitz-type dogs—originally used for work in Arctic regions, these dogs are highly energetic.

■ Sight hounds—these athletic, independent dogs have a strong chasing instinct that needs to be controlled and given an outlet.

■ Scent hounds—many hunting dogs tend to be pack animals and are family-friendly. These dogs need plenty of chances to nose around outdoors.

■ Terriers—bred to tackle small animals, these compact dogs have a feisty nature and a strong digging instinct, which can become destructive if the dog is bored.

■ Gundogs—these friendly hunting dogs are good family pets. Their liking for wet, muddy places can lead to extra grooming needs.

■ Companion dogs—bred mainly for domestic or decorative purposes, most of these breeds are small and easy to keep.

Using the charts

When choosing a breed, consider your lifestyle and home environment—large dogs need plenty of space, and some breeds take longer to train than others. Some dogs need weekly grooming (low), while others need it 2-3 times weekly (medium), or daily brushing (high). Exercise needs also vary from as little as 30 minutes a day (low), 1-2 hours a day (medium), to more than 2 hours a day (high).

WORKING	German Shepherd	Border Collie	Pembroke Welsh Corgi	Rottweiler	Shar Pei	Boxer	Great Dane
SIZE	Large	Medium	Small	Medium	Medium	Medium	Large
EXERCISE	High	High	Medium	High	Medium	High	High
GROOMING	Medium	Medium	Low	Low	Low	Low	Low
TRAINABILITY	Easy	Easy	Very easy	Very easy	Very easy	Very easy	Very easy

SPITZ-TYPE

	Siberian Husky	Samoyed	Norwegian Elkhound	Akita	Chow Chow	American Eskimo	Pomeranian
SIZE	Medium	Medium	Large	Large	Medium	Small	Small
EXERCISE	High	High	Medium	High	Medium	Medium	Low
GROOMING	Medium	High	Medium	Low	High	High	Low
TRAINABILITY	Very easy	Very easy	Very easy	Very easy	Very easy	Very easy	Very easy

SIGHT HOUNDS

	Greyhound	Italian Greyhound	Whippet	Borzoi	Saluki	Irish Wolfhound	Afghan Hound
SIZE	Large	Small	Medium	Large	Large	Large	Large
EXERCISE	Medium	Medium	Medium	Medium	High	High	High
GROOMING	Low	Medium	Low	Medium	Low	Medium	High
TRAINABILITY	Very easy	Very easy	Very easy	Not so easy	Very easy	Easy	Not so easy

SCENT HOUNDS

	Bloodhound	Otter hound	Petit Basset Griffon Vendeen	Beagle	Dachshund (long-hair)	Doberman	Rhodesian Ridgeback
SIZE	Medium	Medium	Small	Small	Small	Large	Medium
EXERCISE	High	High	High	High	Medium	High	High
GROOMING	Low	Medium	Medium	Low	Medium	Low	Low
TRAINABILITY	Very easy	Very easy	Very easy	Very easy	Very easy	Very easy	Very easy

TERRIERS

	West Highland White Terrier	Yorkshire Terrier	Jack Russell Terrier	Airedale Terrier	Border Terrier	Staffordshire Bull Terrier	Miniature Schnauzer
SIZE	Small	Small	Small	Medium	Small	Small	Medium
EXERCISE	Medium	Low	Medium	Medium	Medium	Medium	Medium
GROOMING	Medium	High	Low	Medium	Medium	Low	High
TRAINABILITY	Easy	Very easy	Very easy	Very easy	Very easy	Very easy	Easy

GUNDOGS

	Cocker Spaniel	Portuguese Water Dog	Irish Setter	German Pointer	Weimaraner	Labrador Retriever	Curly-Coated Retriever
SIZE	Medium	Medium	Large	Medium	Large	Medium	Large
EXERCISE	Medium	Medium	High	High	High	High	High
GROOMING	High	High	Medium	Low	Low	Low	Medium
TRAINABILITY	Very easy	Easy	Very easy	Easy	Easy	Easy	Easy

COMPANION

	Pekingese	Shih Tzu	Miniature Poodle	Cavalier King Charles Spaniel	Chinese Crested	Chihuahua	Dalmatian
SIZE	Small	Small	Small	Small	Small	Small	Large
EXERCISE	Low	Medium	Medium	Medium	Low	Low	High
GROOMING	High	High	High	Medium	Low	Medium	Low
TRAINABILITY	Not so easy	Easy	Easy	Very easy	Very easy	Easy	Very easy

The **dog-proof home**

Before you collect your new dog, check your home and yard for things that may cause him harm and remove or put them out of reach to ensure a safe environment for your new pet.

24

Your new dog

Danger areas

The best prevention is to keep a close eye on your dog. Otherwise, to spot potential dangers you need to get down to dog level and do a thorough check for the following possible hazards:

■ Escape routes: a dog can dart through doors, under gates, or down stairs and run into the street.

■ Confined spaces: dogs can squeeze into gaps, such as behind a refrigerator, and get stuck.

■ Poisons: dogs love to eat so this is a big risk. Look out for poisonous plants (humane societies often have lists), toxic chemicals, and even harmful human foods such as chocolate and grapes or raisins (pp.162–3).

■ Things to chew and swallow— cords can cause electrical injuries; sharp objects can hurt a dog's gullet; items such as balloons can cause blockages lower down.

■ Heavy or sharp things—items such as razor blades in the bathroom or garden tools in the shed can cause injuries.

■ Slick floor surfaces—tile or linoleum can be slippery if they (or the dog) are wet.

Outdoor checklist

■ Close off any gaps in hedges or fences or under gates.

■ Move or get rid of toxic plants.

■ Make sure your dog will have shade in the yard.

■ Keep garage or shed doors shut to keep your dog away from machinery, sharp or heavy tools, or chemicals such as antifreeze, paints, and paint thinner.

■ Keep poisons and fertilizers locked up or on a high shelf.

■ Keep your dog away from areas where poisons or slug pellets have been used; dispose of dead animals that have eaten poison.

■ Never leave your dog alone with a grill—hot coals and sharp skewers can cause injury.

DON'T...
leave a grill unattended if you are cooking food.

DO...
keep garbage cans covered and chemicals locked up.

DON'T...
let your dog roam freely except in fenced-in areas, and make sure you close up any holes in fences so he cannot escape.

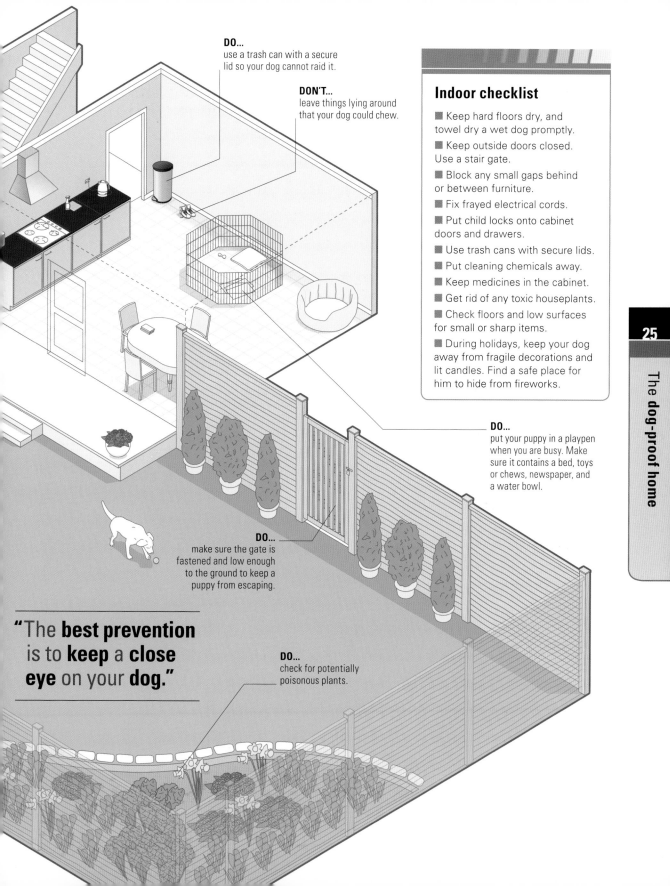

DO...
use a trash can with a secure lid so your dog cannot raid it.

DON'T...
leave things lying around that your dog could chew.

Indoor checklist

■ Keep hard floors dry, and towel dry a wet dog promptly.

■ Keep outside doors closed. Use a stair gate.

■ Block any small gaps behind or between furniture.

■ Fix frayed electrical cords.

■ Put child locks onto cabinet doors and drawers.

■ Use trash cans with secure lids.

■ Put cleaning chemicals away.

■ Keep medicines in the cabinet.

■ Get rid of any toxic houseplants.

■ Check floors and low surfaces for small or sharp items.

■ During holidays, keep your dog away from fragile decorations and lit candles. Find a safe place for him to hide from fireworks.

DO...
put your puppy in a playpen when you are busy. Make sure it contains a bed, toys or chews, newspaper, and a water bowl.

DO...
make sure the gate is fastened and low enough to the ground to keep a puppy from escaping.

*"The **best prevention** is to **keep a close eye** on your **dog.**"*

DO...
check for potentially poisonous plants.

Essential equipment

To ensure that you are ready for life with your new dog, it is best to obtain essential equipment in advance. You can always add extra items once your dog has arrived in your home.

Preparing for arrival

You need to obtain a bed and bowls for your dog before anything else. His bed needs to be big enough for him to stretch out and turn around in. A bed improvised from a strong cardboard box may be fine for a puppy since it can be thrown away if soiled or chewed, or as the dog grows. Molded plastic beds are easy to clean and can withstand chewing. For both types, add a soft lining of towels or blankets. Foam beds are comfortable and many have machine-washable covers. They are good for older dogs with joint issues but not as suitable for dogs likely to chew or soil the bed.

Your dog will need one bowl for food and one for water. Both will need to be cleaned every day; food bowls should be cleaned before each meal. Ceramic bowls are sturdy enough even for large dogs; however, they are often straight-sided, with hard-to-reach corners. Stainless-steel bowls are easy to

> "Make your dog's **bed cozy and** inviting. For a **new puppy,** or a dog who needs **extra security,** use a **dog crate.**"

◁ **Dog bed**
Beds are usually made with high sides for security and a low front so the dog can easily get in and out. Choose a warm, thick lining so that your dog is comfortable.

Dog toys

Toys enable a dog to express natural behavior such as chasing and chewing. You can buy special dog toys like the ones shown here, or improvise your own using items such as an old football or a length of rope. Choose toys made from a material that will not splinter or choke your dog, and are large enough not to get stuck in the dog's throat. To prevent bad habits, do not use old clothes or shoes.

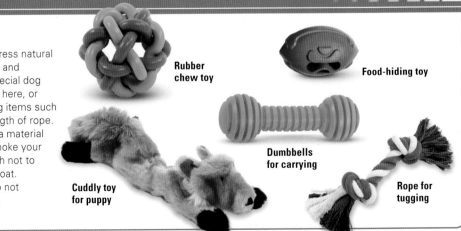

Rubber chew toy

Food-hiding toy

Dumbbells for carrying

Cuddly toy for puppy

Rope for tugging

▽ Choosing a dog bowl

Bowls should be stable enough to stay still during use and shaped so your dog can easily reach into the bottom and around the edges. Ceramic or stainless steel are good choices.

Ceramic bowl

Stainless-steel bowl

△ Puppy crate

Put the crate in a warm, draft-free area where your puppy can see you and other members of the family during the day. It should be large enough for him to move around in.

use and keep clean. The best are non-tip with a rubber rim around the base to keep them still during use. Plastic bowls may be sufficient for puppies and smaller dogs.

You also need to take out pet insurance before taking ownership of a dog. Insurance is essential for illnesses and injuries, and covers costs if your pet is lost or dies, or if he harms a person, other animals, or property.

Home safety

You need to check that your home is safe for your dog (pp.24–5). For a new puppy or a dog who needs extra security, it can help to use a dog crate—a large pen with wire sides and top and a solid base. Line the base with newspapers in case of accidents and add bedding and toys. A crate must be a comforting "den" for your puppy. It is a good

place to keep him until he is toilet-trained, for short periods if left alone, or as a safe space if he is hurt or ill. Never leave him in the crate for long periods, or lock him inside as a punishment.

Grooming and hygiene

You will need a basic grooming kit (pp.50–1) even for short-haired dogs including a bristle-haired brush or a rubber-toothed mitt. Dogs with long or thick coats may need a long-bristled brush, round-ended scissors for trimming hair, and detangling spray; your vet or a breed society can guide you. You will also need shampoo and a towel for bathing your dog, and perhaps nail clippers.

For clearing up dog droppings outdoors, carry small biodegradable bags. Vets and pet stores sell bags specially made for this purpose.

Collars and leads

Use a soft fabric collar for a pup, fastened so that you can slip two fingers between it and the pup's neck, and check every week that it is not getting too tight. For adult dogs, use fabric or leather collars, or a harness for a strong dog. Avoid metal choke chains. Attach a name tag to your dog's collar, giving your contact details.

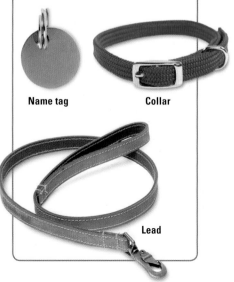

Name tag   **Collar**

Lead

Bringing your dog home

Introducing a new pet into your home will be exciting but perhaps a bit nerve-racking—and not just for your dog. Prepare as much as possible beforehand and plan for the first day at home to be quiet and calm.

Being prepared

Make sure your home is "dog-proofed" (pp.24–5) and that you have bowls and bedding ready for when the dog arrives (pp.26–7). Have at least a week's supply of food and collect any diet sheets and initial supplies from the breeder or animal shelter.

Select a "den" area for the dog during the day—somewhere warm and quiet but where your pet can see and hear people so he will not be lonely. Place your puppy crate in this area if you are using one (p.27). Have newspapers ready to put on the floor in case of accidents.

> "**Introduce your dog** to your home **slowly** so that he can **get used** to his **new environment.**"

If you are getting a young puppy, letting the pup sleep in a box or basket in your bedroom can help him to settle in. You need to have a name ready. Choose a name of one or two syllables as this will be easy for the dog to learn, but avoid any names that could be confused with words you might use to command the dog such as "stay" or "no."

Arriving home

As soon as you get home with your dog or puppy, take him into the yard since he may want to relieve

△ **Let him explore**
Your dog might like to sniff scents and look around the yard. Allow him to do so since it will help him relax and habituate better to your home and the new surroundings.

himself. Then let your dog into your house and let him explore. For the first day at least, keep your pet in his den area so he can get used to the home slowly. A puppy will probably tire quite quickly so allow him to sleep whenever he wants.

Meeting family members

Introduce your dog to everyone in the family. If you have children, supervise them for the first few days as they and the dog get used to each other. Explain to the children in advance that your new

△ **Settling down**
For the first few nights, your puppy may feel more secure if he is sleeping in a box in the bedroom. Speak to him gently if he whimpers but don't make a fuss of him.

dog may be feeling a little nervous so they need to be quiet around him. To meet the dog, have the children come into the room with him and sit down quietly and give them treats to offer him. Say that they need to let the dog come to them of his own accord. Explain that the dog will enjoy playing with them but they have to keep play sessions short for the first few days so he does not get overexcited or tired. They must not grab the dog or pick him up suddenly or he could get frightened and bite them.

▽ **Introducing a baby**
Let your dog meet the baby once he has settled in. Show the baby how to stroke the dog gently, then let the baby try.

Meeting other pets

Let your new dog meet other pets one at a time after the first day or so, once he has settled in.

Introduce resident dogs to the new one in "neutral territory" such as the yard so there is room to escape if one of them gets nervous.

◁ **Making friends**
Introduce a new dog to a resident dog in a toy-free area, then buy new toys that the dogs can share once you know that they are getting along well together.

Make a fuss of your resident dog before paying attention to the new one to reduce any risk of jealousy.

To introduce a cat, choose a large room or the yard and hold on to the dog while the cat comes to meet him. Make sure the cat has an easy escape route in case the dog gets too boisterous. Never feed cats and dogs together since the dog may try to steal the cat's food. If you have rabbits or other small animals, keep them in a cage and supervise the dog whenever he is around them.

The **first few days**

Take things quietly for the first few days to let your dog settle in and get to know his new home. Make sure there is always at least one member of the family around to keep an eye on him.

Getting into a routine

Establish a routine from day one—feed your dog and take him outside to relieve himself at regular times. Set the ground rules for what your dog is allowed to do and where he is allowed to go. For example, if you don't want your dog to go upstairs or lie on chairs or beds, teach him this rule right from the outset.

Getting used to the home

Introduce your dog to any noisy or potentially frightening household machines such as the vacuum cleaner and washing machine. Let him be present while the machine

△ **Getting confident**
For a puppy, a new home can be a very scary place. Get him used to noisy appliances like the vacuum cleaner so that as he grows he becomes confident in the human world.

◁ **A regular routine**
Take your puppy or dog outside to relieve himself at regular times—whatever the weather. A set routine will help him to avoid having accidents in the house.

> **"Establish a routine** from **day one—feed your dog** and **take him outside** to relieve himself at **regular times**. Set the **ground rules** for what he can do."

△ **Keeping your dog entertained**
If you have to leave your dog alone in the house, leave a toy with him to keep him entertained and occupied while you are gone.

▷ **Separation training**
Start by leaving your dog for a couple of minutes at a time, a few times a day, and gradually extend this as he accepts being alone.

is running but at a comfortable distance with an "escape route" if he needs it. If your dog looks nervous, get down to his level and speak to him in a gentle, encouraging tone, or distract him with a toy until he seems calmer.

House-training

Dogs instinctively avoid soiling their "nest" area, and this is a useful basis for toilet training. Bear in mind that there may be a few accidents in the house before your puppy is fully trained.

Developing a routine will help avoid accidents. Take your pup outside after eating, when he first wakes up after a nap, just before bedtime, and just after any exciting event (such as meeting a new person). You may need to take a young pup out about once an hour. Keep to his toileting times as closely as possible. Watch for signs

that your pup needs to "go" such as sniffing the ground, turning in circles, and squatting. If you notice any of these, take him out immediately. Stay outdoors with your dog until he relieves himself. As soon as he does so, give him lots of praise.

Home alone

Being alone is stressful for dogs; if they are not trained to tolerate this, they can become destructive or noisy, or may have accidents in the house. Your dog needs to learn that he will be safe on his own and trust that you will return.

To begin training, choose a time when the dog is calm or even sleepy. Start by leaving him in his pen or a room for just a few minutes. When you come back in,

don't make a fuss of him; just stay nearby quietly until he calms down. Extend the periods gradually until he can be left for several hours without becoming stressed.

When you go out and leave your dog at home, make sure he has access to his bed and a bowl of water. Also give him a toy with food hidden in it to keep him occupied for a while after you have left.

Socializing your dog

Your puppy will need to get used to people, cars, and the outside world. Training may also be necessary for an older dog who lacks confidence or has behavioral problems outside the home.

Local walks

Once your puppy has been inoculated and microchipped, he can be taken for walks. It is important to expose young pups to as many different situations as possible. Once puppies reach 12 weeks, their attitude becomes more guarded, and if they encounter something strange their first instinct will be to run away.

▽ **New faces**
Walks are a great way for your dog to meet people that he may not normally see, such as toddlers and teenagers. You can use toys and treats to make these encounters more fun.

For older dogs, walks are about letting them get to know their "territory." Even so, there may be things that your dog has not encountered before such as livestock and wild animals.

Creating confidence

When your dog first ventures into the wider world, the experience can be overwhelming for him. Some things may be frightening such as cars and trucks. Others may be powerful distractions: for example, a toddler on a tricycle or sheep in a field could trigger your dog's chasing instinct. Your dog needs to learn confidence—and you need to be sure you can depend on him to behave in all situations.

Introduce your pet to anyone who wants to meet him. If you have children, meet them from school with your puppy so he gets used to seeing other children.

When acquainting your dog with other dogs, start with those you already know. You could arrange "puppy play dates" at home or go out for walks with someone who has an older, easygoing dog. If your dog is upset by strange dogs, walk

Getting used to traffic

■ Introduce your dog to startling or distracting sights such as noisy cars by getting him to sit at a comfortable distance while the vehicle goes by.

■ Crouch down and hold him so he does not try to chase, and praise him when he sits quietly.

■ Reward him with a treat once the object has passed.

■ Gradually get him used to being closer to these objects but at a safe distance from fast traffic.

■ Be patient—let him take his time.

▷ **Comfortable journeys**
Make sure your dog has space to lie down and turn around comfortably in a car. If using a dog guard, your dog can be left free in the back. Use a blanket or pillows to make him comfortable.

away from them or ask the owners to hold their dogs or put them on the lead while you pass.

It is best to keep your dog on a lead around livestock and wild animals—even for a quiet dog, the temptation to chase can be sudden and irresistible. In many countries, dog owners have a legal duty to prevent their animals from harassing livestock.

Get your dog used to distractions such as motor vehicles, bicycles, and people on roller skates or skateboards (see box, left).

Traveling by car

As a dog owner you have a legal duty to transport your dog in a way that keeps the dog and other vehicle occupants safe. If you have a large car, you could fit a dog guard behind the rear seats; this should be sufficient for short journeys under one hour. For long trips or in a larger vehicle, put your dog in a dog crate. If your dog is traveling on the back seat of your car, a dog harness that links in with the seat belt system can restrain him safely.

Start travel training by teaching your dog to sit in the car for a few minutes with the engine off and the doors open. Graduate to sitting in the car with the doors closed and engine on for a few minutes. Then start taking short journeys of a few minutes, building up to longer trips.

When traveling, don't let your dog stick his head out of the window since he could risk head or eye injuries. For long journeys, carry water and a bowl and stop at least every two hours for your dog to have a drink and to get out and relieve himself. Switch on the air conditioning if your car has it, and never leave your dog alone inside a car even with the windows ajar—on a warm day or in direct sunlight, heat stroke can kill a dog in as little as 20 minutes (pp.166–7). Watch for any signs of travel sickness such as drooling or panting. Excessive barking or chewing on the car's interior are other signs of distress. To help prevent these, make sure your dog has a nonslip surface to stand on in the car.

Going on vacation

Nowadays there are an increasing number of "dog-friendly" vacations available for you and your pet. If you do need to leave your dog though, there are also options to ensure he is well cared for while you are away.

Your new dog

Traveling together

Traveling with your dog can be fun —with a bit of prior organization. Your dog needs to be controllable in public places and trained for car travel (p.33). He also needs to be microchipped and wear an ID tag.

If you plan to travel abroad with your dog, find out what regulations apply to taking dogs into that country and if there are any legal rules regarding car travel with dogs; animal welfare organizations may have information on these issues. You may need to have your dog vaccinated for diseases such as rabies. Arrange travel insurance for him. Find out how the airline or ferry company usually transports dogs. Ferry companies may provide open-air kennels on deck or air-conditioned spaces inside the vessel. Airlines may require your dog to travel in a special crate, and they also have transport rules for dogs. Check in advance that your destination will be dog-friendly.

Take a good supply of your dog's usual food, and familiar items such as food bowls. Keep to your normal routine of feeding, walks, and bedtimes as much as possible to minimize stress.

△ **Comfortable car journey**
Your dog should have enough space to move and stretch during a car journey, especially if the journey is likely to be several hours.

▷ **Meeting a pet sitter**
If you decide to leave your dog at home, let him meet any potential sitter so that you can assess how well the sitter gets along with him.

▽ Family kennels

If you have two dogs, check with the boarding kennels that they have a kennel big enough to house both dogs together. It will reassure your dogs to stay together and help them settle into the new environment.

△ **Exercising safely**
Some dogs are not fond of other dogs. Let your sitter or kennels know if your dog will accept being exercised with other dogs, and whether he is particularly shy or strong-willed, which could affect how he gets along with strange dogs.

Leaving your dog behind

If you do not plan to take your dog with you, there are several ways to arrange care while you are away. Whichever option you choose, you need to be sure your dog is used to being separated from you (p.31).

You could ask a relative, friend, or neighbor to "pet sit," or employ a registered pet sitter. It is advisable to leave your dog with this person rather than alone in your home. If you can, arrange a few visits to the pet sitter's home in advance so that it becomes a familiar place to your dog. Make sure your dog will be wearing an ID tag at all times. Leave a good supply of his food

with the sitter, plus notes on feeding, walking, and bedtimes, and emergency contact numbers for you and for the vet. If you plan to use a registered sitter, ask your vet or fellow dog owners for suggestions on suitable people, and ask the sitter for references.

Another option is to use boarding kennels. Your vet or other local dog owners should be able to recommend good ones. Staying at kennels can be more stressful for your dog than staying in a home environment. It is wise to visit the kennels before using them to see whether they will be suitable (see box right). Remember to book well in advance, especially at busy times of year and if the kennel is a popular one.

Boarding kennels

When assessing kennels, you need to check that they have the following:

■ License from a local authority.

■ Environment: the kennels and common areas should be clean, warm, draft-free, and secure. Each kennel should have a raised platform that your dog can lie on or under.

■ Feeding: staff should keep to your dog's usual foods and feeding times.

■ Handling and exercise: dogs should get attention and exercise at least twice a day.

■ Veterinary care: access to 24-hour care.

"When **traveling abroad**, check **in advance** that your **destination is dog-friendly.**"

2

Everyday care

A **balanced diet**

Dogs need more than just meat—they need a healthy, balanced diet and the right quantity for their size. Most people buy prepared dog food, but you could make your own if you prefer.

Essential elements

A good diet should provide all of the nutrients that a dog needs and must contain these elements:

■ Proteins—the "building blocks" of cells, proteins help to build muscles and repair the body. Lean meat, eggs, and dairy products are good sources of proteins.

■ Fats—high in energy and making food more tasty, fats also contain essential fatty acids, which help to maintain cell walls and aid growth and wound healing in your dog. They are the source of vitamins A, D, E, and K, and are found in meat, oily fish, and in oils such as linseed oil and sunflower oil.

■ Fiber—found in potatoes, vegetables, and rice, fiber helps to bulk up food and slow your dog's digestion, allowing more time to absorb nutrients and making it easier for him to eliminate.

■ Vitamins and minerals—these help to maintain your dog's body structures such as skin, bones, and blood cells, and support the chemical reactions that turn food into energy or enable vital body functions such as blood clotting.

■ Water—as with humans, water is essential for your dog's life. Make sure your dog has access to fresh water. Refill the bowl with water two or three times a day.

Commercial foods

These foods can be moist, semi-moist, or dry. Dry foods can help keep teeth and gums healthy, but check that they have wholesome core ingredients. You must provide plenty of water too, since dogs who are fed dried food drink more. Moist foods have a lot of moisture content along with higher fat and protein components.

The advantages of commercial foods include a wide choice of brands; foods made for specific

◁ **Healthy diet**
Your dog's energy level, his life span, general well-being, and behavior all depend on the type of food he eats.

▷ **Varieties of food**
The choice of foods available for dogs has greatly expanded. This ranges from specially developed commercial foods —moist, dry, or semi-moist—to natural foods that can be prepared at home.

Moist food

Dry food

Natural food

△ **A good choice**
Rawhide chews are a safer alternative to real bones. They are also useful to help occupy your dog when he is left alone for periods at home.

Give a dog a bone?

Vets advise against giving dogs bones because they can cause blockages in the digestive system. Never feed cooked bones since these can splinter and injure your dog's mouth or gullet. Instead, choose bone-type treats or chews made of rawhide, which can keep his teeth healthy and satisfy the urge to chew but without the risks of real bones.

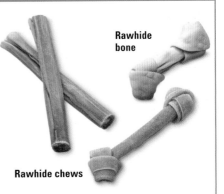

Rawhide bone

Rawhide chews

groups such as puppies, seniors, and pregnant or lactating females; clearly defined nutritional values; and ease of use. However, these foods can contain ingredients such as preservatives and flavorings that could disagree with your dog. Check the labels on these items if you are unsure of the ingredients, and look at the websites of pet food standards organizations for guidance.

Natural foods

Instead of feeding your dog a packaged diet, you can prepare a homemade, natural diet in the form of raw meat. You will also need to add cooked vegetables and starchy foods such as rice to provide fiber, and check with your vet if you need to add a vitamin and mineral supplement.

This diet is closer to how a dog might eat in the wild, and you know there are no preservatives or other hidden extras. However, natural foods need to be carefully balanced and it can be difficult to ensure consistent nutritional quality or to

adapt the diet to different energy needs of dogs. Preparation of fresh food on a daily basis can also take a lot of time.

Treats and chews

Many dog owners give extra tasty foods when training or simply as a treat. Some treats can be high in fat, so if you give them to your pet regularly, make sure to reduce his main meals to prevent overeating. You can buy treats at pet shops or make the treats at home. Dogs prefer smelly and soft treats that have more meat in them, so try giving your dog treats with foods such as cheese and chicken or sausage in them.

▷ **Dog treats**
There are many different types of tasty treats you can give your dog, and they are useful rewards for good behavior. Try out different treats to see which one he likes best. Only allow your dog a few treats each day though to avoid overfeeding.

Chews, on the other hand, help keep your dog busy, preventing him from chewing household items such as shoes and furniture, or biting your hands. Chews are especially good for puppies during teething. They also play an important role in keeping your dog's teeth clean and help keep his jaws in good condition.

> "A **natural diet** is **closer** to how a dog might eat **in the wild.**"

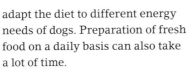

Cooked sausage

Cheese cubes

Moist treats

Meaty treats

Bite-sized treats

Monitoring feeding levels

As with humans, animals can develop health problems due to overeating or a poor diet. Make sure your dog eats the right amount of food to maintain an optimal weight for his breed or size.

Good feeding habits

The way you feed your dog is as important as what you feed him:
■ Set regular meal times.
■ Make sure you wash the food bowls before every use.
■ Clear away food bowls when your dog has finished eating, especially if feeding moist canned or homemade foods.
■ Don't feed your dog the same things that you eat—his needs are different, and some foods for humans, such as chocolate, can be poisonous to dogs (pp.162–3).
■ If you need to alter your dog's diet, make changes gradually to avoid any stomach upset.
■ Check that fresh drinking water is available at all times.

> **"Do not feed** your dog **scraps** from the table, and **never give in** to **begging** for **food."**

Eating too fast?

It is natural for a dog to eat fast; in the wild, this would keep other pack members from stealing his food. If your dog gobbles his food too quickly, try using an anti-gorge bowl. This has lumpy protrusions in the base that your dog has to work around as he eats, slowing his rate of eating. This can help prevent digestive problems such as gas, vomiting, and indigestion.

Preventing obesity

Some dog breeds are prone to put on weight, such as the Basset Hounds, Cavalier King Charles Spaniels, Dachshunds, and Labrador Retrievers. However, any dog can get fat with too much high-energy food and too little exercise. Overfeeding your dog can lead to heart problems, diabetes, and painful joints. In particular, for breeds that have large bodies and thin legs (such as the Rottweilers or the Staffordshire Bull Terriers), weight coupled with exercise can cause ligament problems. To prevent weight problems:

△ **Anti-gorge bowl**
The anti-gorge bowl does not allow dogs to take large bites of food since they must eat around the molded shapes. This results in a slower, more relaxed feeding time.

Lumpy protrusions

■ Feed for your dog's age, size, and activity level (pp.42–3).
■ Be extra vigilant about feeding treats to your dog; don't feed scraps from the table, and never give in to begging for food.
■ Ask your vet about a balanced diet for weight loss.
■ Weigh smaller dogs at home on bathroom scales. If your dog is large, ask your vet's office if he can be weighed there.
■ Keep an eye on your dog's body shape—this can be just as helpful as weighing him. You can even take photos every week to monitor any changes in his weight.

A healthy weight

You need to check your dog's condition regularly to ensure that he is not too fat or too thin. Body shapes differ between breeds, so find out what is normal for your dog's breed. If you are not sure about the right quantity to feed, ask your vet.

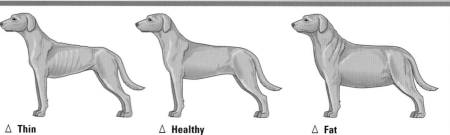

△ **Thin**
The face looks thin, the ribs easily felt or seen, and the tummy more drawn in than normal for the breed.

△ **Healthy**
The fur is shiny, the body is well-muscled but not bony, and there's a slight waist.

△ **Fat**
The tummy is large, there are rolls of fat at the back of the neck, and a thick layer of fat over the ribs.

The right portion
Always feed a balanced diet to your dog, consisting of carbohydrates, proteins, and fats. Research the correct meal size for your dog's size, age, and activity level.

Dietary change through life

Dogs at different stages of life have particular nutritional needs—whether growing puppies, nursing mothers, sport dogs, or older pets. It is important to ensure your dog has the right nutrients for health and energy for his age.

Puppies

Once puppies are weaned, they need to be fed little and often—four times a day at first, going down to three times a day at about six months. Puppies grow fast so they need high-energy food; ask your vet if you are unsure of the right quantity to feed your pup based on his size. Increase the amount slowly as he grows, but avoid overfeeding since this can lead to obesity in later life. It may be best to feed commercial puppy food to make sure your pup gets the right balance of nutrients.

If you have bought your puppy from a breeder, he may supply a sample of the food that the pup has been eating. Stick to this food in the beginning and introduce changes gradually.

Adult pets

For many dogs, two meals a day (morning and evening) are enough. Neutered dogs need fewer calories than unneutered dogs; otherwise, feed according to your dog's size and activity level. Monitor your dog's weight regularly to make sure you are giving him the right amount of food.

Working dogs

Working or sport dogs should have high-protein, energy-dense, easily digestible foods to maximize their strength, speed, and stamina. However, the volume of food given to a working dog should be no more than for a normal adult dog. Different types of work require different energy sources:
■ For short, fast bursts such as racing or agility shows, dogs need a moderately increased fat intake.
■ For endurance work such as sledding, hunting, or herding, dogs need high-fat foods with extra protein.

△ **Growing up**
Always provide your puppy with a well-balanced diet to build a strong body. Be sure to choose food that is specially formulated for puppies and change to an adult formula as your puppy matures.

▷ **Fit for the job**
Working dogs such as the Collie, which are bred for their strength and stamina, require a diet rich in proteins and fat to keep them energetic while they carry out endurance work.

Climate considerations

Dogs in colder climates need more energy than those in warmer regions in order to keep their body temperature stable. The same applies to dogs living in outdoor kennels as opposed to house pets. Regular meals that are high in fat calories can fulfill their additional daily energy requirements.

△ **Nursing needs**
The nutritional requirements of a nursing mother are even more than that of a growing dog. Her calorie needs will steadily increase as the puppies grow and she produces more milk to feed them.

"For many dogs, **two meals a day** is **enough. Feed** according to **size** and **activity level.**"

Nursing mothers

A pregnant dog can stay on her usual diet until the last two to three weeks of pregnancy; from this point until whelping, her energy needs will increase by 25–50 percent. She may lose her appetite as the time to give birth approaches—this is normal. Her appetite will soon return after the puppies are born. A dog producing milk will need two to three times as many calories than normal in the first four weeks, when the puppies' milk needs are at their highest. Feed her energy-dense food such as puppy food or working-dog food, and feed little

and often. By the time the puppies begin weaning (at six to eight weeks), the mother will still need extra calories until she has stopped producing milk altogether.

Convalescent dogs

A sick dog will need easily digestible food such as boiled chicken and rice; your vet can help give you guidance. Some companies make extra-nutritious, palatable food for convalescent dogs. Feed your dog little and often, and ensure the food is warm so it will be more tempting. Keep a note of how much your dog is eating, and report any loss of appetite to the vet.

Older dogs

From about age seven onward, dogs start to need more nutrients but fewer calories. Many do well on a normal adult diet, slightly reduced in quantity and with vitamin and mineral supplements (ask your vet about these). Some dog food companies produce "senior" formulas that are softer, palatable, and with higher protein, lower fat, and extra vitamins and minerals. You may need to adjust feeding to three times a day. A slower metabolic rate makes older dogs more prone to obesity. Keeping a healthy weight can improve the quality and length of your dog's life.

Fighting fit

All dogs need exercise or they can become bored and frustrated. Regular sessions daily will help your dog burn off excess energy and also help him to stay calmer at home and accept periods of being left alone.

Daily exercise

Dogs need at least two exercise sessions per day. For puppies regular exercise can help to build strength and reinforce learning, while for older dogs gentle activity can help to prevent problems such as obesity and painful joints. Dogs bred for hunting and working have higher energy levels than other breeds (see breed table on pp.20–3); two half-hour walks might be plenty for a Yorkshire Terrier or a Pug, but a Dalmatian or Boxer might need an hour-long walk or run plus a training or play session.

If your dog is under exercised, he can develop behavioral problems—he may become hyperactive and agitated and find it difficult to settle. He may also find alternative, destructive outlets for his mental and physical energies such as chewing up household furniture, barking excessively, or running away to look for entertainment.

Exercising your dog can be built into your daily activities: for example, taking the dog with you when you collect your children from school or walking him to the local store. You could also find open areas where your dog can play or explore, or set up an exercise space in your yard. The following tips will help to keep him comfortable when exercising:

■ Watch that your dog does not get too tired: have "warming up" and "cooling down" periods such as 10-minute slow walks at each end of the exercise session.

■ On hot days carry water with you and exercise when it is cooler, in the early morning or evening.

> **"Regular exercise** can help your dog to **build strength** and **reinforce learning."**

△ **Exercise partners**
Going for a jog or run with your dog is great exercise for you both and can be a part of your usual daily routine.

▷ **Family fun**
Exercising your dog with the whole family can be a great deal of fun and will help build a strong bond with your pet.

△ **Active life**
Dogs with high energy levels need plenty of exercise and play to stay calm and happy. They need open areas where they can run free, especially when they are young.

■ In cold weather consider using a dog jacket for short-haired or elderly dogs to help keep their muscles warmer.

■ Don't let your dog run on hard surfaces if he is not used to it since he could hurt the pads of his paws. Similarly, avoid these surfaces if they are very hot or cold.

■ Take your dog's favorite toy or ball out on walks with you to encourage fun and energetic games of fetch. These fun games are also good mental exercise for your dog.

■ Try to keep sessions at around the same time each day so that your dog learns to rest in between.

Walking and jogging

This type of exercise can be done almost anywhere. Jogging with your dog will help you both to keep fit. For his own safety and that of others, your dog needs to be able to walk calmly on a lead (pp.72–3). Remember to carry bags with you to collect and dispose of droppings.

Free running

Running in open spaces is especially good exercise for high-energy or racing dogs such as Whippets and Greyhounds. First, in order to trust your dog to run a long distance from you, he needs to be trained to come reliably when you call him (pp.74–5). Find a large space such as a field or a beach without crowds. Check that there is no other animals that he could disturb. Make sure you are allowed to let your dog run freely in that area—many parks don't allow dogs off leads in certain places.

To ensure that your dog keeps his eye on you while he is running around, play a few games of "hide and seek" or "fetch" with him (p.76). Agility games such as jumping over and running through obstacles can also be great exercise for your dog (pp.88–9).

Age and exercise

Your dog's need for exercise will change through his life.

■ Young pups can start going out once they are inoculated. Keep exercise sessions short.

■ For adult dogs, long walks, runs, and energetic games are ideal. Pregnant dogs, or sick or convalescent dogs need only short, gentle exercise sessions.

■ Older dogs appreciate shorter, gentle walks, but may still enjoy learning new games.

Time to play

Dogs are intelligent animals, and play is very important for stimulating their minds. Playing with your dog can build your relationship, reinforce his training, and also help him learn how to get along with other dogs.

Types of games

Games can allow your dog or puppy to express his natural instincts in a fun way. Puppies who learn to play with other dogs are less likely to be timid or aggressive. Dogs particularly enjoy playing fetch, tug-of-war, and squeaky-toy games.

Fetch Chasing a ball or Frisbee is an excellent way for your dog to burn off energy. By bringing the toy back to you, the dog learns that he will get another try at chasing—and in the process he learns retrieval skills (p.76). Use toys rather than throwing sticks—your dog could injure his mouth by catching a stick in the air or grabbing at a stick embedded in the ground.

Tug-of-war This game can be fun for both dogs and people, but bear in mind that "challenging" a person can sometimes become a bit too exciting for your dog. Use special "tug" toys (p.26). Make sure you win more often than the dog does. If he takes hold of your clothes or skin, stop playing immediately and quietly turn away from him.

◁ **Fun exercise**
For games of fetch, take toys with you when you go for walks rather than using sticks. Playing "fetch" also encourages your dog to come to you when called.

Tips for play sessions

The following tips will enable you and your dog to get the most out of your play sessions:

■ Keep play sessions short and varied so your dog will not get tired or overexcited.

■ Make sure you decide when the play session starts and ends—this subtly reinforces your position as "pack leader."

■ Remember that all toys are yours—dogs should always give up their toys when asked.

■ Never encourage your dog to chase people. Humans should be friends and leaders, never "prey."

■ Prevent play biting while your puppy is small—teach him to play with toys instead.

■ Never let your dog jump up at people or grab things from them.

◁ **Tugging away**
Tug of war games are a favorite with many dogs—especially terriers and competitive dogs. Dogs enjoy the energy release and feelings of strength that the game evokes.

■ Toddlers can be unnerving for dogs since they may cry loudly and move quickly and erratically. Gently prevent your toddler from grabbing at the dog, and make sure the dog can escape.

■ Explain to children that puppies tire easily and must be allowed to sleep if they want to.

■ Dogs do not like to be disturbed while they are eating. Don't let your children play with or near a dog's food or water bowl. Only an adult should feed a dog.

■ As well as play, involve older children in training your dog. With the right support, children make skilled and enthusiastic trainers.

Hide and seek This game satisfies a dog's food-seeking instincts. Hide a bit of food inside a toy, so your dog has to scrabble and sniff around to find it, or take several plastic cups and hide some food under one of them. You could also play hide and seek with two people: one person takes the dog's "fetch" toy (such as a ball) and hides with it, while the other holds the dog. The "hider" calls the dog, and the other person lets the dog go. When the dog finds the hider, this person throws the toy for him. This game is also a fun way to teach your dog to come when called.

Squeaky toys Dogs bred to catch small prey, and those with a strong predatory instinct such as terriers, enjoy playing with squeaky toys. The squeak signifies the cry of an injured animal and is especially appealing to chase and catch. Some dogs may even chew the toy until it stops squeaking, so make sure the toys don't have small or sharp parts that could cause choking.

Children and play

Dogs and children share a sense of fun and love of life, and they can become the best of friends but they need time to get habituated to one another. Children can be a little too rough with dogs while playing, so all play and interaction between them should be supervised. Avoid a situation where your dog is forced to retaliate and be ready to step in to help when required. The following guidelines should help ensure everyone has fun safely:

■ Explain to your children that playtime can be fun but they must not tease a dog because this will upset him and he may bite.

△ **Playing together**
Children are full of enthusiasm and fun and can make very good trainers. Well-socialized dogs respond to them with excitement and energy and enjoy their play sessions.

> **"Games** can **allow your dog or puppy** to express his **natural instincts** in a **fun way."**

Tug of war
Games involving tug toys are great fun for dogs, whether playing together or with their owner. Playing a friendly game with another dog teaches your puppy important social skills such as cooperation and tolerance.

Washing your dog

An occasional bath can be great fun for your dog, especially if you get him used to it from an early age. Bathing is essential for a dog's skin and coat and keeps dirt, smells, and hair shedding to a minimum.

How often you should bathe your dog depends on what type of coat he has. Some long-haired dogs have a "double-coat" with a warm undercoat and thick guard hairs on the top. The guard hairs make double-coated dogs naturally dirt repellent, so they don't need to be bathed very frequently— twice a year is enough. Single-coated, short-haired dogs should be bathed more frequently—about once every three months. Curly coated dog breeds like

Poodles do not shed their hair, and may need to be bathed more regularly, even as often as once a month. It is important not to wash any dog too often, as over-bathing causes the coat to compensate by producing extra oils, which in turn causes an increase of natural odor. If your dog gets muddy after a walk, he does not necessarily need a bath—just wait until the mud dries and then brush it off.

1 △
Prepare for bath time
Lift your dog into the bath, then spend some time feeding him treats to make sure he is happy before you get him wet. Make sure you have dog shampoo, a towel, and a brush within easy reach so that you don't have to leave your dog unattended.

2 ▷
Wet the coat
Test the water temperature before you start to wet your dog—it should be warm, but not hot. Beginning at the head, wet your dog fully from head to tail, being careful not to get water into his eyes, ears, and nose.

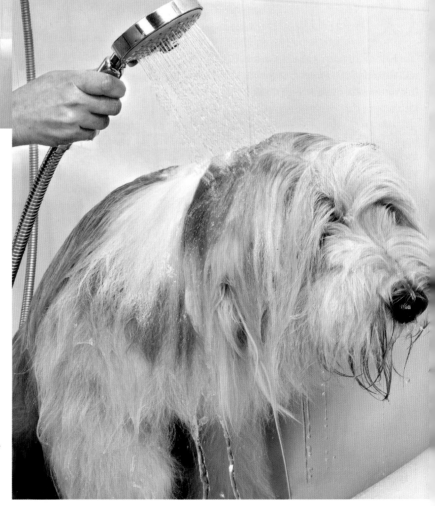

3 ▽ ▷

Shampoo and massage
Apply dog shampoo and then massage it thoroughly into your dog's coat, right down to his skin.

4 ◁

Rinse the shampoo out
Use warm water to thoroughly rinse all the shampoo out of your dog's coat. Any shampoo residue left in the coat will cause skin irritation.

5 △

Dry the coat
Squeeze the excess water out of your dog's coat with your hands, then towel him all over, so that he is nearly dry. Finish by drying him fully with a hair dryer on low heat—as long as your dog isn't worried by the noise—brushing as you go.

Bath time
In warm weather, it may be easier to wash your dog outside rather than in the house. Use warm water and a specially-formulated dog shampoo, and dry him right away to keep him from getting cold.

Long-haired dogs

Dogs with long coats require more grooming than dogs with short coats. Essential tools for keeping their coats in good condition include a slicker brush, rake, comb and dematting comb, and scissors.

Long-haired dogs should be groomed daily to stop tangles from forming. Some breeds, such as Afghan Hounds, have extremely thin, silky hair, which tangles easily and forms knots. Others have hair that cannot fall out due to the length of the coat, causing it to form thick mats. Regular grooming will allow you to avoid these problems—you cannot rely on occasional trips to a professional groomer if you have a long-haired dog. Not only will your dog start to smell and look messy between visits, but removing the matted hair that builds up can be very painful for him. You will find it easiest to groom your dog when he is tired after a walk.

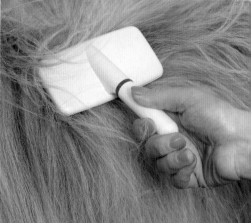

1 ◁

Dematting comb
Mats can be difficult to remove and may cause pain to your dog because you will inevitably pull some hair out while removing them. To make dematting easier, begin by breaking the mats into smaller manageable sections with a dematting comb.

2 △

Slicker brush
Once all of the big mats and knots have been removed, use a slicker brush to go over your dog's coat until there are no tangles left. Pay particular attention to the feathering around his legs.

4 △

Comb around the face
Leave your dog's face until last, then spend some time carefully combing through the hair around the muzzle. A well-groomed dog will leave very little dead hair in a comb, which should pass through the coat easily.

3 △

Rake the coat
Pick an area of coat, hold the rake lightly in one hand, and brush smoothly through the coat. Work systematically from head to tail along one side of your dog and then back up the other side.

"Long-haired dogs should be **groomed daily** to stop **tangles** from forming.**"**

Trimming around the feet (for long- and short-hair)

Hold the scissors flat against your dog's pad, then trim the coat so it is level with the base of the foot.

Then turn the foot over to trim around its top edges. Comb and trim the hair between the toes.

Short-haired dogs

Although they require less attention than long-haired breeds, short-haired dogs still benefit from regular grooming. A shedding blade and hair dryer are both effective for removing dead hair from a short-haired dog.

Short-haired dogs can be kept in perfect condition with just a two-minute daily brush and a thorough groom once a week. For your weekly session, start by using a hair dryer on a low heat to remove the dead hair from your dog's coat. Work in a systematic fashion to make sure no part of the coat is overlooked. Then use a shedding blade to pick up any remaining hair. Brushing should stop when all loose hair is removed from the coat—that is, when it becomes difficult to remove more than half a brush full of hair. If you like, a damp towel or coat conditioner can then be used to add shine to the coat.

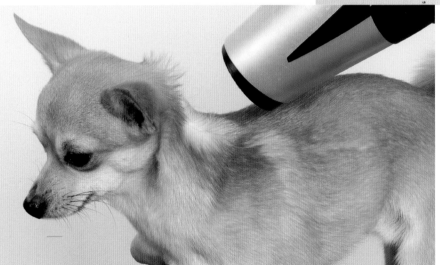

1 △
Bathing
Short-haired dogs only need an occasional bath—about once every three months. They can be easily bathed at home; use a non-slip mat to keep your dog secure.

Using a hair dryer
Hair dryers are an effective way of removing dead hair and dirt from short-haired breeds, though some dogs do not like the noise. If you use a hair dryer, it should always be on a low heat.

Shedding blade
A shedding blade will pick up any remaining dead hair from your dog. Pass the blade lightly over the whole of his body, pressing gently and working with the direction of the coat.

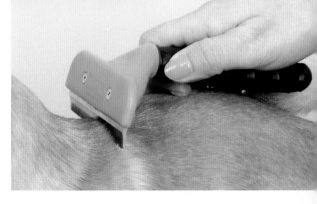

4

The finished product
Regular grooming means you and your dog will both benefit from a clean, odor-free coat that sheds very little hair.

Wiry- and curly-haired dogs

Many owners of dogs with wiry and curly hair choose to take their pet to a professional dog groomer. Alternatively, you can learn the necessary skills to groom your dog at home.

Hand stripping

Hand stripping is a method where the dog's hair is plucked from the root by hand. It is used for certain types of wiry haired breeds—typically working dogs such as Border Terriers and also for some show dogs. It is a very time-consuming method that is not always necessary for pet dogs. Hand stripping is best done when the dog's coat is naturally shedding, or "blown." This normally happens twice a year, and makes the process much easier and less stressful for the dog. Many experts prefer to use their fingers to pluck a few hairs at a time from across the whole coat. However, there are several tools available to make the process easier on both groomer and dog, such as a pumice stone, hand-stripping knife, shredder, and scissors.

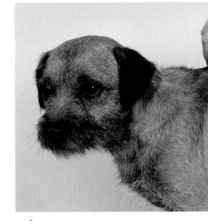

1 △
Pumice stone
The coarse texture of a pumice stone makes it perfect for removing the rough hairs from a dog's top coat. The stone should be gently dragged over the top of the coat in the same direction as the hair.

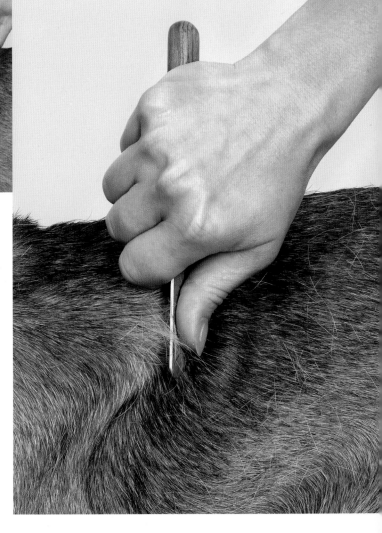

2 ▷
Hand-stripping knife
This is an excellent tool that can be used to remove the coarse topcoat from wiry coated breeds but is also used to "card" the undercoat—stripping out the shedding hairs quickly and easily.

Everyday care

3. ▽
Shredder
There are many types of shredders available, some with large flexible blades and others with fixed teeth. In essence this is a serrated blade for removing the loose undercoat hair, while leaving the top coat intact.

4. ▷
Scissors
Once all of the shedding hair has been removed, a dog can appear quite ragged. It is best to finish grooming by trimming his extremities to even out the coat. Then use thinning scissors to trim the finer hair around his legs and face.

Clipping

Clippers are an essential tool for grooming non-shedding, curly-coated breeds such as poodles. Many types of clippers are available, but the more money you spend, the higher quality you can expect. Clippers take training and practice to use correctly. They should be held lightly between thumb and fingers, like a pencil. The amount of pressure you use and the position of the clippers should remain constant, otherwise the coat will be different lengths. Clipping should be done after a bath when the coat is clean and dry, because a very dirty or oily coat is impossible to clip.

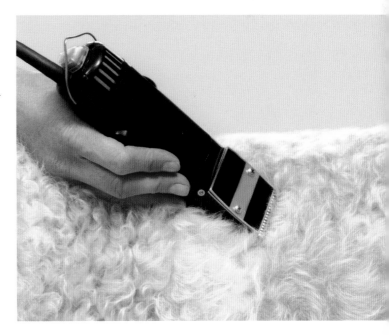

▷ **Using clippers**
Choose a clipper blade appropriate for your dog. A "number 5" blade is a good overall choice and leaves the hair about ½in (1cm) long. Using clipper guards may be a safer choice for an inexperienced groomer since there is less room for error.

Other grooming needs

It is not just your dog's coat that needs attention—his teeth, ears, and nails also need to be attended to regularly in order to keep your dog healthy and in the best possible condition.

Everyday care

Teeth cleaning

Dog's teeth benefit from weekly brushing, though you should only use dog-specific products. First, get your dog used to the feeling of having your hand resting across the bridge of his nose, with your thumb held under his chin to keep his mouth closed. Once he is comfortable with this, use your other hand to gently lift his top lip to reveal his teeth. If your dog remains calm, a toothbrush or fingerbrush can be inserted inside the cheek.

Teeth cleaning will be a strange experience for your dog at first, so use treats at each stage to put him at ease and encourage good practice in future. If he shows signs of aggression or anxiety during the process, stroke him slowly and gently for several minutes before trying again.

◁ △ *Teeth brushing*
The most important place to brush is along the gum line, as well as on the outside surfaces of all the teeth. Move the brush gently in a circular motion rather than scrubbing from side-to-side. You might find it easier to use a fingerbrush—a hollow plastic tube that fits over your finger and has in-built bristles. This can be a lot easier to maneuver around your dog's mouth and prevents you from applying too much pressure.

"Teeth cleaning may be a **strange experience** for your dog so put him **at ease."**

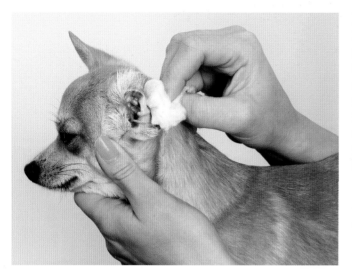

Ear cleaning

Inspect your dog's ears regularly for any signs of discharge, unpleasant odor, redness, inflammation, or ear mites. Any of these symptoms may signal an infection, for which you should seek veterinary help (pp.114–115). Monthly ear cleaning will maintain the health of the ears and prevent infections. This is particularly important for dogs with ear flaps such as Spaniels.

◁ **Applying antiseptic ear cleaner**
Antiseptic ear cleaner can be applied to a cotton ball and used to wipe the visible areas of your dog's ears. Do not insert the cotton ball or any other object into your dog's ear canal.

Nail trimming

How often you will need to trim your dog's nails depends on his lifestyle and the dog itself, but monthly trimming should be enough for most. Nails need to be trimmed back as far as the "quick," which is where the blood vessels and nerves are. If you cut the nails too short, severing the quick, the bleeding may be extensive and can be difficult to stop.

Hold your dog's foot firmly to keep him from moving while trimming his nails. Place the nail clippers just below the quick and cut the nail swiftly in one smooth movement. If you do cut the quick, remain calm and apply a small amount of styptic powder to the nail, applying firm pressure until the bleeding stops.

◁ **Black nails**
Dogs with black nails present a challenge since the quick can only be seen as a small white dot in the center of the nail once you begin to trim. Trim only small sections at a time to prevent cutting through the quick.

△ **White nails**
The quick is much easier to see on dogs with white nails than on dogs with black nails. It is a two-tone pink area in the center of the nail, so make sure you clip below this point.

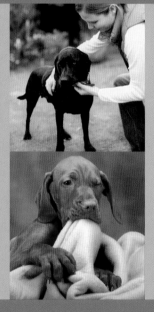

3

Training and behavior

Being in charge

Having a well-behaved dog depends on building a good relationship with him. Learning to communicate the rules in a clear and calm way that your dog understands will ensure he responds positively to your requests.

Setting rules

Dogs are not naturally misbehaved, in fact they are deeply social animals who crave boundaries and rules. However, puppies are not born knowing what the rules are, and even if you are starting to train an older dog, he may not yet have learned all the rules you would like him to follow. Decide upon a set of rules you feel are important, then enforce them consistently through training methods such as reward-based training (p.69). Act quickly to stop any behavior that breaks your rules; your dog will soon learn which behaviors are acceptable and which are not.

There is no need to prove your physical strength or dominance to enforce these rules. A good owner is calm, fair, and likable—it is important to help your dog understand when he makes mistakes without getting angry and shouting at him. Building a relationship with your dog based on mutual respect will make both the owner and the dog happier.

Your dog will gladly follow commands given by you as long as he understands what he needs to do. When training problems occur, it is usually because of poor communication. Since dogs have different motivations and needs than humans, taking time to understand how your dog learns and what signals he can follow will help set realistic expectations.

△ **Happy together**
A healthy relationship is one where your dog is at ease because he knows what is expected of him as a pet, and where you enjoy the company of a dog who does as he is asked.

◁ **Clear communication**
Being a good dog owner is about learning how your dog interacts with the world and training him in ways that he is able to understand.

△ **Avoid confusion**
If you give a voice command at the same time as a hand signal, your dog will tend to learn the hand signal but ignore the voice command.

Voice and hand commands

Your voice is a useful training tool, but it is easy to forget that dogs cannot understand spoken language. Your dog is capable of remembering what certain words sound like and what he should do when he hears them, but only after repeated training and only if those words always sound the same. Asking your dog to "sit" one day and "sit down" the next will confuse him and make training more difficult. The tone of your voice is also very important. Your dog will use your tone to gauge whether he is doing the right thing or not, so always keep your voice cheerful when teaching new words.

Your dog will also look at your body posture to work out the context of a situation and what you are asking him to do. However, just as dogs have no concept of language, they do not understand that by pointing at something you are trying to direct their attention to somewhere other than the end of your hand.

Dogs and especially puppies find learning hand signals easier than learning voice commands—

△ **Staying focused**
Don't get angry if your dog gets distracted by his environment. Instead, do something to turn his attention back to you. Using treats or a toy, even a game of chase, will all help to re-engage him.

only a small part of their brain can process verbal information. Once your puppy has learned the hand signal and is responding reliably to it every time, add a voice command ahead of the hand signal. Eventually, after lots of repetitions, your dog will respond to the voice command alone.

Remember, your dog can only concentrate on one thing at a time. Be patient while training and ensure that your dog has fully learned one command before trying to teach him a new one.

Pack behavior

Dogs are pack animals and, like humans, they seek out social companionship and build strong relationships. Also because their ancestors once lived in packs, dogs look up to a leader they can respect and follow. Without a firm leader they may misbehave. Giving approval through praise and affection will make your dog feel secure and loved. If he senses you are angry or distracted, he may become fearful or withdrawn.

Basic training

Training should be an enjoyable experience for both you and your dog. These pages will get you started, but if you are unsure, always seek the help of a professional dog trainer sooner rather than later.

When to train

There are many things to consider while training, but the most important is to choose the right time. Aim to train for a few minutes several times a day since this will get much better results than a longer training session once a day. Choose times when you are not stressed or in a rush, otherwise your dog will sense your tension and be far more likely to get things wrong when trying to please you.

Equally important is to consider your puppy's mood. Trying to train an overexcited puppy who hasn't had much exercise will be difficult. And a puppy who has just eaten a large meal will feel sleepy and will not be particularly motivated by food treats. Start training him in a quiet, distraction-free environment such as your living room, especially when attempting to teach new or difficult commands. You may want to build up to training in high-distraction environments such as

"Training your dog involves **creating a situation** where he is **rewarded** for **certain behaviors** instead of others.**"**

◁ **Indoor training**
Begin training indoors away from distractions of the outside environment. When you do move training outside, start somewhere quiet and enclosed, far from other dogs and people.

△ ▷ **Treats or toys as rewards**
Treats should be small, soft, and smelly. They work best when they can be given quickly during training sessions and do not take your dog several minutes to eat. Favorite toys also make a great reward for playful dogs.

a local park but do not attempt this until your puppy has had plenty of practice already.

Reward-based training

Training your dog involves creating a situation where he is rewarded for certain behaviors instead of others. Any behavior that is consistently rewarded will be repeated more often. This also means that bad behavior, which is not rewarded, will soon disappear and be replaced by one that is rewarded. For your dog to understand how you want him to behave, give or withhold a reward at just the right time. Rewards can include food treats, games with toys, simple praise and affection, or even playing with other dogs. Remember that not all dogs find the same rewards appealing. Spend some time discovering what really

motivates your dog and use that as a reward. Giving a reward immediately following the behavior you want means you will never need to use punishment to motivate while training.

One of the easiest reward-based ways of training is to use a food treat to lure your dog into the position you want him to be in. More complicated behaviors can be broken down and rewarded in stages, in a method called "shaping." So if you want your dog to sit, every time he moves closer to the ground and you reward him, he will realize what he is being asked to do. Getting rewarded for each small effort will make him repeat it. Maximize your training success by limiting his choices and thus preventing him from making the wrong decision. For example, train on a lead away from other dogs or in a room with no distractions.

Carry your dog's rewards with you whenever you plan to do some training. There is also a lot of

equipment you can buy to help you during training such as collars, leads, and harnesses. Choose equipment that is comfortable for both you and your dog to use, and ask a professional to help you fit and use it correctly. However, always remember that while good equipment is necessary during training to keep your dog safe, avoid relying on tools too heavily. The day that you forget the equipment or it breaks, it will be the good training you have done that will prove most important.

Sit and stay

The most basic of training but also the most useful—the sit and stay commands—can help you control your dog in any situation. Most training and behavior problems can be improved by teaching a reliable sit on command.

Sit

Dogs naturally sit of their own accord, and it can be quite easy to simply reward them as and when it happens. However, taking the time to teach your dog to sit on command ensures he sits quickly and reliably in the face of any distraction. It is one of the easiest commands to teach, and one that any dog will readily learn.

1 ◁
Dog in a stand
Hold a treat in front of your dog's nose when he is standing in front of you. Lure him by moving the treat over his head so that he raises his nose.

3 ▽

Introduce hand signal
Once your dog learns to sit, teach him to respond to a clear hand signal—an upward motion with a flat hand with palm facing up. After several repetitions, say "sit" a moment before the hand signal.

2 △

Feed treat and praise
When your dog folds into the sit, release the treat and praise gently. Continue to praise and feed him treats if he remains sitting for longer.

> **"Sit is one of the easiest commands to teach, and one any dog will readily learn."**

Stay

Once your dog has learned to sit on command, teach him to "stay," with your hand flat and palm facing down. You will feel more confident in an emergency situation if your dog obeys "sit" and "stay." These commands also help control unwanted behaviors. Unlike most basic training, teaching your dog to stay for long periods is best practiced when he is tired, since he will be happy to rest in one place and more likely to remain still.

2 ◁
Insert movement
When your dog has learned to stay reliably, slowly move away from him by taking a step back and leaning your weight onto your back leg.

3 ▽
Add distance
Move around your dog while he is sitting. If he moves to you, calmly reposition him and repeat. Gradually build up the distance away from him.

1 ◁
Ask for sit
Ask your dog to sit, then hold your palm down and say "stay." Praise him immediately.

GOOD PRACTICE

After your dog has mastered the sit and stay, gradually teach him "down." From a sitting position, first lure him by bringing the hand with the treat in it all the way to the floor so that your dog follows it. As soon as his elbows are both on the ground, reward him immediately. Once he is reliably going straight down, introduce a clear hand signal—a downward motion with palm facing down—and again lure him into the down position. The next step is to train him to respond to your voice. Say "down" and then give your hand signal.

▷ **Make him feel safe**
Only ask your dog to lie down in environments where he feels safe, since dogs tend to feel vulnerable in the down position.

Walking on a **lead**

All dogs need to be walked on a lead at least some of the time to ensure their safety. Teaching your dog to do this without pulling will make going for a walk a more pleasant experience for you both.

Teaching a puppy to walk on a lead without pulling is easier than teaching an adult dog, who may have learned all sorts of bad habits. However, no matter when you start the training, it is crucial to set rigid ground rules. As soon as your dog pulls, stop walking and help him into the correct position by your leg. This can be very frustrating to begin with since you will be stopping every few paces. But by following the steps outlined here you can teach your dog where you want him to walk and reward him when he gets it right.

1 ◁

Position the dog
Lure your dog into position using a treat in your left hand. Keep the treat low enough so he doesn't jump up, and the lead short enough that he can't wander off.

2 ▽

Step forward
Keep your dog's attention by saying his name cheerfully and hold him in position against your leg, sitting or standing, with the treat.

3. ▽
Treat in position
Take a step forward, stop and let your dog have the treat while he is in the correct position. If he stays by your side, take another step forward and reward him again.

4. ▷
Practice
With each session, gradually increase the number of steps you take before rewarding your dog. If he moves away from you or gets distracted, lure him back

GOOD PRACTICE

Each new environment is likely to prove challenging for your dog, so start each training session by rewarding one step at a time. As he gets good and is walking nicely for a few paces, progress to working with distractions in the distance such as other dogs. If he starts pulling or loses attention entirely, he probably isn't ready for this stage yet. Move the training to a quieter area and go back one stage.

Never get cross with your dog if he makes mistakes. Teaching him to walk without pulling takes time, and you should plan longer walks to allow for the many stops you will have to make. Some dogs, especially older rescue dogs, are really dedicated "pullers," and basic training may be unsuccessful. In such cases it is best to seek the help of a professional dog trainer.

Resist the urge to use collars that tighten around your dog's neck. They do not teach your dog anything and have the potential to cause him serious damage.

▷ **Come close**
When training in a new environment for the first time, use special treats that your dog finds particularly tempting.

Come when called

The most joyful times you can have with your dog are outside, watching his enjoyment as he really stretches his legs. However, until your dog will reliably come when called, it is not safe to let him off the lead.

Training your dog to come when called should not be started on walks because there are simply too many temptations that may cause your dog to ignore you. However, by practicing the following simple steps at home or in your yard, your dog will learn that coming back to you is always the better choice.

1 ▷
Show the treat to tempt him
Get your dog focused on you by tempting him with his favorite treat. Let him sniff the treat but have a friend gently hold his collar so he can't reach to eat it.

2 △
Call him
Keep your dog's attention on you and take a few paces away from him, then crouch down to your dog's level, throw your arms wide open, and call him with an enthusiastic "come." As you do this, your friend can let go of your dog's collar.

GOOD PRACTICE

Do not be tempted to call your dog over great distances to begin with since he may get distracted; he needs to be close enough to stay fixated on the treat.

However, if he doesn't come back to you immediately, do not enter into a game of chase with him. Simply walk away and try training again later.

No matter how long it has taken your dog to come back to you, never correct him when he does come back. He will not understand that you are angry because he has taken so long, he will only learn that coming back to you is a bad idea!

Once your dog has learned to come every time you call him, you can gradually stop giving him his favorite treats and just use praise instead.

△ "Come to me"
Your dog will learn to respond to your body language, so always keep your arms wide and welcoming when calling.

3.

Encourage him with a treat

As soon as your dog is within a couple of feet of you, hold out the treat as a lure and tempt him to come right up to you. Tease him a bit with the treat—you don't want him to grab the treat and run off.

"Good boy!"

4.

Reward and praise

As you feed him the treat, gently take hold of his collar with your other hand and tickle his chin. Praise him and feed him some more treats so he learns that coming back to you is really beneficial.

Fun training

Training does not need to stop at obedience commands such as sit. Some of the most fun training you can do with your dog involves teaching games such as fetching toys or learning amusing tricks.

Fetch

One of the most enjoyable games for a dog to learn is how to fetch a toy on command. It also helps him get good exercise without your having to move. No dog is born knowing how to retrieve, so it's necessary to teach him the rules of the game first.

Build excitement
Start by holding your dog's favorite toy. Make lots of enthusiastic noise and tease him by moving the toy around.

Throw the toy
When he is really interested in the toy, throw it a short distance in front of him so that he races to get it.

"Good dog!"
Praise your dog as soon as he picks the toy up but do not try to take it from him. This will only make him want to run away to play with his prize on his own. Give him even more praise, and even a food treat, if he returns the toy to you.

Wave

Teaching tricks is a great way to bond with your dog and keep him interested in training. Giving a paw, which is easily turned into a wave, is a great trick and will impress any visitors. Keep sessions short and always go back a step if your dog jumps up, and praise and reward even the slightest attempt to wave. Once he has mastered waving, develop it into the high five (see panel, below).

1 △

Giving a paw
Hold a treat and make a fist so that your dog can smell the treat but cannot reach it. Put your fist on the floor and encourage him to investigate. Praise any attempt to use his paw.

2 △

Move fist up
When your dog understands he has to touch your hand with his paw to release the treat, slowly move your fist away from the floor.

3 ▷

Wave
Over successive training sessions move your fist higher and higher so your dog has to reach his paw up and "wave" to earn the treat.

GOOD PRACTICE

When your dog is performing these tricks confidently, introduce a voice cue by giving a command a moment before giving your hand signal. Continue to use treats until he is reliably responding to your voice cue alone. Teach him to distinguish between the voice cues of the wave and the high five (see right).

Once your dog can wave or high five confidently with you kneeling in front of him, try teaching him to respond to your commands while you stand. Reward your dog well each time he gets it right.

▷ **High five**
Turn the wave into a high five by stretching out your hand. As your dog lowers his paw, let it land against your palm. Support the paw lightly rather than holding it as he may find this threatening.

Training classes

Training classes are an excellent way to teach your dog good behavior. They are also a good way to meet other like-minded people and learn about the facilities your local area has to offer dog owners.

When to consider classes

No matter what your experience of training dogs, classes are advisable for any new dog—whether it be a puppy or an older, rescued dog. The benefits dogs receive from taking part in a group class are enormous, and it is also a good way to hone your skills. All dogs are different and will benefit from slightly varied approaches in their training. Furthermore, having an experienced trainer on hand will prevent you from making mistakes. It is also much easier to keep motivated when training as part of a group.

However, nervous dogs and those who are aggressive toward people or other dogs are not suitable for group classes. These types of behavioral problems are often aggravated in a class situation and can become more pronounced. Quite often these dogs are better off starting in a one-on-one training session, with someone who is qualified in dealing with behavioral problems, before progressing into a group class. If you have any concerns, inquire before enrolling your dog.

Where to train

There are likely to be several classes offered in your area. Try to get recommendations from other dog owners or your vet. Choose a trainer who is recognized by an official organization such as the Association of Pet Dog Trainers. Before you choose a class, take the time to visit and watch a training session take place. Even if you have no experience with training classes, you will quickly get a feel for a good class. Aim for classes with relaxed dogs and happy owners. Avoid hectic and noisy environments.

What to look for

- Smaller classes with fewer dogs.
- High trainer-to-dog ratio.
- Positive training methods utilizing praise, food, and toys.
- No choke chains.
- No aggressive training.
- A relaxed environment.

> "The **benefits dogs** receive from taking part in a **group class** are **enormous,** and it's a **good way** to **hone** your **skills.**"

◁ **Training classes**
Training classes should be well organized and enjoyable for all the owners and dogs present. A knowledgable and experienced trainer will take charge in a friendly and effective manner.

Obedience heeling
All training classes teach the basic skill of getting your dog to heel when walking. If you can keep your dog by your side in a controlled environment, you will soon be able to walk him in public spaces with confidence.

Behavioral problems

Most dogs who are trained in basic rules from a young age happily integrate into their household. However, some dogs develop unwanted behaviors throughout their lives that require further training.

Destructive behavior

Chewing is a natural behavior in dogs, but when it becomes excessive or is targeted toward something inappropriate, it can quickly become a source of tension between an owner and their dog. There are some common reasons why a dog may become destructive. For example, puppies will naturally chew on things out of curiosity, and this behavior becomes more pronounced while they are teething. However, this tendency disappears with age and consistent training. Sometimes dogs become destructive as an outlet because they are experiencing physical pain or because they are suffering from a genuine separation anxiety disorder. Much like humans, dogs can develop mental illnesses, however supportive and happy their home life. Separation anxiety in dogs is a recognized condition characterized by extreme distress during the absence of their owner. It is imperative that advice about this condition is sought from your vet in combination with a professional behavioral therapist.

Occasionally, destructive behavior such as chewing or digging can become a problem in otherwise healthy, adult dogs. Quite often this is a sign that the dog is not being sufficiently stimulated or may not have an outlet for the behavior elsewhere and is feeling frustrated. Terriers, for example, have been bred to dig, and allowing them to exhibit this behavior by searching

◁ **Dealing with chewing**
Puppies naturally use their mouths to investigate their environment, but you should never punish them for this or they will learn to hide from you when they are chewing.

▽ **Biting problems**
Puppies "play bite" humans in the same way they do other puppies, and this is best discouraged early on. If your puppy gets too excited, simply walk away.

for treats in a particular area—such as a sandbox—can save the rest of your yard. This will only work when all of their other needs such as physical exercise, nutritional requirements, and social interaction are met.

Problem solving

In order to tackle such destructive behaviors, first you must decide how you are going to allow your dog to perform the behavior in an acceptable way. For example, a dog that chews furniture can be taught to chew special toys containing food instead.

The first stage of training is to highlight to the desired behavior by associating a command word with the behavior. For example, offer your dog a toy with some treats hidden inside and praise him as he begins to investigate it, telling him, "Good boy, chew," in a clear voice. During this training it is vital that you make some temporary changes to restrict your dog's opportunities to perform the unwanted behavior. If the behavior you are trying to eliminate is chewing furniture, do not allow your dog to wander in the house unsupervised. If that is impractical, look into other

△ **Chew toys**
Chew toys, some of which can hold treats, can be used to tackle a huge range of problem behaviors. It is wise to get your puppy used to having quiet time with their toys every day.

preventives such as a bitter spray to make the furniture taste unpleasant.

When you have made a good association between the cue word and the correct behavior, you have a channel of communication when your dog misbehaves. Resist the urge to punish your dog in this situation. He is not being naughty —he just needs to chew and cannot be expected to know the difference at first between your furniture and his toys. If you catch him chewing the furniture, simply interrupt him (for example with a hand clap) and hand him his chew toy, saying, "Good boy, chew."

"A dog that **chews furniture** can be **taught** to **chew his toys** instead."

Barking and jumping up

The most common behavioral problems associated with dogs are barking and jumping up at people. Both of these can be very cute in puppies but soon become irritating when they extend into adulthood.

Training and behavior

Barking

Excessive barking is a behavior that can quickly become a problem within a household and can cause tension with neighbors, too. As is so often the case with commonly occurring behavioral problems, barking is a completely normal dog behavior. They are genetically predisposed to do it and therefore it is unfair to expect a dog never to bark. However, it is perfectly reasonable to teach them to bark in moderation and only in certain circumstances. Bear in mind that dogs sometimes bark incessantly when shut in a room or in the yard for long periods. In this case, your dog's routine should be changed to allow them more freedom, which will result in reduced barking.

The easiest way to control problem barking is to train your dog to bark on command and follow this with teaching "be quiet" on command as well. Teaching a dog to "speak" is a great game and one that most dogs who already like to bark take to very quickly. Start by doing something that would normally cause your dog to bark, such as waving a toy or knocking at the door. When you have discovered a reliable way of encouraging your dog to bark, insert the command to "speak" just before they bark. Praise them for barking and then approach them

◁ **Beware of the dog**
Dogs will often bark at people or other dogs passing their territory. Although their intentions may be friendly, this can appear intimidating to some people and should be discouraged.

△ **Anti-barking measures**
If your dog persistently barks at passersby or strangers in his territory, then try pulling curtains across windows to restrict his view.

▷ **Don't pay attention**
Do not give your puppy any fuss or attention if he jumps up. Only praise him when he has all four paws on the floor again.

and hold a treat in front of their nose to stop them from barking. Then simply say the word "quiet" and feed them the treat. Training sessions can be repeated several times throughout each play session, and are best ended with a fun game of fetch or tug-of-war.

Never start this training, however, if your dog is barking out of aggression. If your dog barks sharply at people or other dogs, this is an aggression issue (p.85), and it would be wise to seek help from a professional behavioral specialist.

> "Save **time** and **effort** by **teaching** young **puppies** not to **jump up** from the **first day** you **bring them home.**"

Jumping up

Jumping up is probably the most commonly complained about behavioral issue and is the one problem that owners are most guilty of creating themselves. Puppies naturally tend to jump up to try to get closer to people's faces and hands, which they recognize as the sources of affection from humans. It is natural to encourage this because it seems cute and fun when puppies do it. However, before long they will have doubled in size and their habit of jumping up becomes annoying, painful, and potentially dangerous. It is possible to save a lot of time and effort later on in life by teaching young puppies not to jump up from the very first day you bring them home.

However, if you have an older dog who already habitually jumps up at people, you will need to train him that this is unacceptable. This can be as simple as following the instructions to teach a "sit" (p.70).

A dog that is sitting cannot jump up and therefore the problem is solved. In practice, if the urge to jump up is irresistible to your dog, it may be necessary to set up specific training sessions to solve the problem. To do this, put him on a short lead and get a friend to walk slowly toward you. When you have your dog sitting obediently, your friend can approach and give him praise but must move away again if he gets overexcited and jumps up.

As training progresses, you should be able to take off the lead but your dog will still need to be reminded to sit. It is imperative that everyone enforces the rule not to let him jump up or your training will fail. Do not make the mistake of becoming complacent when praising your dog for sitting obediently. If he is not getting any praise for sitting politely, he is very likely to jump up as a way of getting lots of attention again.

Running away and aggression

Despite your best efforts, it's possible that your dog might develop a serious behavioral problem. The most common and potentially dangerous examples are a dog that runs away and a dog that responds to situations aggressively.

Running away

All dogs love being able to run free, really stretching their legs and playing with toys or other dogs. However, until your dog will return when you call, it is not safe to let him off his lead. You may come across someone who isn't confident around dogs or perhaps meet another dog who is not friendly. Often dogs learn to run away from their owners because they have been allowed to play off the lead before they have properly learned to come when called. Dogs habitually run away from their owners for a variety of reasons. Do not take it personally, simply remind yourself that your dog spends all day in a house with you and is finding the temptations of the outside world too distracting. In this case it is likely that your dog views returning to you as a signal that his fun is about to end and is therefore best avoided. If your dog finds running away more rewarding than staying with you, training must focus on ensuring your dog not only comes back to you but also enjoys spending play time with you.

If your dog will not return to you in a distraction-free environment such as your home or yard, it is too much to expect him to come back on a walk. Go back to basics and practice "come when called" at home in a quiet environment (pp.74–5). You can introduce recall training to many elements of your daily life; try recalling him to a food bowl at dinnertime, or recall from a thrown toy. Remember to always give lots of praise when he comes back to you.

Once your dog will return to you quickly and happily in and around the house, it is time to move the training outside. Walk your dog on his normal lead, but have a light, long lead attached as well and tuck it away in your pocket. When you get to a safe, open space you can

△ **Runaway dog**
The outside world can be full of temptations for your dog. You should always practice recall training with your dog in a quiet, controlled environment at home before you let him off the lead during walks.

▷ **Returning for treats**
Dogs should be taught that coming back when called means that they get a reward and are then allowed to continue playing. Only occasionally does it signal the end of the walk.

Aggression

Aggression is a natural canine response when a dog is not comfortable in a situation. However, for pet dogs to be trustworthy in all situations they must understand that aggression is not an acceptable response toward humans or other dogs. By the same logic, a good owner needs to take note of when a dog is becoming distressed and take steps to help him be more comfortable in that situation, thus reducing the risk of an aggressive response in the first place. However, most happy and well-socialized dogs are not aggressive other than in rare cases where they are injured and in pain or surprised while sleeping.

Never challenge an aggressive dog. If a dog is growling at you, they are telling you that they are unhappy and want you to move away. Pinning them to the floor, shouting at them or any other harsh treatment will only result in the dog becoming more aggressive over time as they feel the need to defend themselves.

> "**Aggression** is a **natural canine response** but it is **rare** in **happy**, well **socialized** dogs."

make a big show of taking your dog's lead off. He will assume he is off the lead, but in actual fact you have hold of the end of the long line. Do not use this as you would a lead—it is simply your safety line. You should aim to leave it dragging along the ground and avoid it pulling taut. Now try calling your dog as you have practiced at home: say your dog's name, followed by "come," stand up tall and wave your arms with a big smile on your face! Your dog should want to come back to you, because he knows he will get treats or praise every time he does.

Keep the training varied—ask him to come many times and be totally unpredictable with when you call him. Give him treats sometimes, play with him others.

Occasionally put him back on the lead for a little while and then let him off for a free run again. Keep him with you for a minute or two, then next time call him and send him running off again. The key is to always praise the recall in some way.

Controlling risks

Aggressive dogs are not only a risk to you and other people but also to fellow dogs. Do not attempt to remedy the problem without professional help. First, ensure you put control measures in place, such as keeping your dog muzzled and on a lead when out, and then speak to your vet about getting a professional, accredited dog behavioral therapist to assist you.

Taking the lead
When training your puppy, it is important to have clear rules in place to ensure he knows what is acceptable behavior. With patience and persistence, even a badly behaved pup can be taught good manners.

Competitions and sports

Becoming involved in further training provides fun and satisfaction for both you and your dog while strengthening your bond. There are many sports you can take part in and competitions you can enter with your dog.

Dog shows

There are a number of different activities to choose from but before you start make sure to register with the appropriate governing body and familiarize yourself with the rules. Many people choose to first enter their dogs in a breed show. However you may be discouraged if your dog does not do as well as you think he should. You can improve your chances of success by finding a good training class run by experienced breeders and handlers from the show world. In many parts of the world there are also companion dog shows, which tend to be smaller and less daunting shows for beginners.

An alternative to breed showing are less competitive, pet-friendly obedience competitions. Dogs are required to perform a series of obedience tasks such as walking on a loose lead and going to their bed. These competitions are usually structured by levels of increasing difficulty, and dogs are judged on their ability to complete tasks including heeling, stays, retrieve, and recall. Dogs who earn a gold award are recognized as being very obedient.

When looking for a local obedience club to train with, be sure to find one that uses only positive training methods like those outlined in this book.

Agility

An increasingly popular alternative to standard obedience competitions is canine agility. Dogs learn to negotiate a range of obstacles, and winning requires a high level of training skill as well as speed. Dogs never seem to tire of jumping over hurdles or through hoops, running through tunnels, weaving through poles, and balancing along a seesaw. Success depends on the amount of practice you are prepared to put in with your dog, and many competitors own their own agility equipment or attend a training club several times a week. Canine agility is not recommended for young puppies because their

△ **In tandem**
Dancing to music is enjoyed both by dog and owner. It requires the dog to be fit and supple and to work in perfect harmony.

◁ **Wonderful win**
The pleasure of winning your first award with your dog is something you will remember for many years to come.

growing bones and joints can be damaged by jumping. Dogs need to be at least 18 months of age to be allowed to compete.

Variations

As dog sports have become more popular in recent years, several variations on obedience and agility training have appeared. Rally obedience (Rally-O), with its informal feel and variety of freestyle exercises, is emerging as a favorite sport. Unlike traditional obedience competitions, handlers follow a predetermined route as opposed to following the judge's orders and they are allowed to encourage their dogs. Yet another alternative is freestyle and heeling to music—otherwise known as dancing with your dog. With practice the routines can look

△ **Weave poles**
Weave poles are one of the most difficult obstacles for dogs to master. It requires them to weave in and out rapidly without missing any of the poles.

△ **Tunnels and jumps**
Tunnels vary in height and style with some placed in such a way that the exit is not visible to the dog. Jumps also vary and require dogs to judge distance and height carefully.

> **"Dogs never seem to tire of jumping over hurdles or through hoops, running through tunnels, and weaving through poles."**

extremely impressive with jumps, twists, and turns, and even walking on two legs. However, in essence these are obedience moves taught one at a time and put together to fit a music track. There are many beginner's courses available at training clubs to get you started.

An increasingly popular alternative to agility is flyball, which involves teams of dogs racing each other and jumping over

hurdles to press the flyball box. This action releases a ball, which the dogs must then return to the start. Flyball suits toy-oriented, social, and energetic dogs who enjoy retrieving. For those dogs not suited to working as part of a team, there are disc sports such as Frisbee-catching. Dogs earn marks for catching the Frisbee over increasing distances and even earn extra points for style.

Trials and events

Working and gun dog field trials take a high degree of training but are a hugely rewarding way to release your dog's potential. Not all dogs are suitable, so if you are interested it is worth speaking to an expert first.

Working trials

These field trials are loosely based on the training police dogs undergo and appeal to many trainers due to the variety of exercises and less formal assessment involved. Dogs must progress through increasingly difficult challenges to move up to the highest level. All of the tasks are divided into control, agility, and nose work categories.

The control round includes heel, retrieve, speak on command, send away, stays, and steadiness to gunshot. The agility stage involves jumping a hurdle and long jump as well as scaling a wall. The nose work is split between a search square—where dogs must locate any object carrying human scent within a given area—and a tracking exercise. Tracking is where a dog follows the path walked by a person, possibly several hours before. The dog is required to use his nose to detect ground particles or any other disturbance left by the track-layer.

Gun dog trials

If you own a gun dog breed such as a Labrador Retriever your dog is likely to love bringing objects back to you. Gun dog trials or field trials (which are very similar but do not actually involve shooting game) test a dog's ability to fulfill the role of a working gun dog. Tests include flushing and retrieving game as well as the necessity for gun dogs to remain under control around guns at all times.

Other events

There are a variety of other niche sports suitable for particular breeds, such as water rescue events for Newfoundland dogs and their crosses; racing for Afghan Hounds; tracking tests for Bloodhounds; and carting for Bernese Mountain Dogs.

There are also many different endurance events for all breeds but only the most fit and active dogs can participate. These activities include dog hiking, canicross (cross-country running with your dogs), joring (biking or skiing with your dogs), sled-dog racing, and protection sports such as *Schutzhund*, where dogs are taught to search out and apprehend "criminals." All of these sports will improve your dog's physical and mental well-being. But more importantly, the enjoyment you will both receive from working together is immeasurable.

△ **Herding**
Dogs that are bred to herd livestock will often develop behavioral problems if they are not given a suitable outlet for their herding instincts. Herding trials are perfect for these breeds.

▷ **Sled dogs**
Many dog breeds were created for the sole purpose of pulling sleds. Sled dogs such as Huskies get huge satisfaction from doing what they were bred for.

Gun dogs
Unlocking your dog's true potential will be a real thrill for both him and you. Gun dogs take naturally to the work, since they are bred specially for this reason. The real skill is inserting control and enthusiasm.

4

Your **dog's** health

Signs of good health

A healthy dog is easy to recognize by the way he looks and behaves, allowing for individual variation, breed, and age. Once you get to know your own dog, you should have no difficulty in judging if all is well.

Healthy appearance

Bright eyes, a glossy coat, and a cold, wet nose may be cited as classic signs of good health in a dog, but these are not invariable rules. A dog's bright eyes may dim with age, even if he stays perfectly fit; his coat will not look glossy if it is wire-haired; and a healthy dog can have a warm, dry nose.

Perhaps more useful fitness indicators are your dog's body shape and weight, which should stay consistent: strange swellings, sudden loss of weight, and abdominal bloating are all possible early health warnings. Monitor weight gain and growth in a young dog by weighing him weekly and plotting the weight on a graph;

back up this data by taking regular photographs as he matures.

Changes in health are also revealed in a dog's feces and elimination habits, which can be markedly different from one dog to another. As you clean up after your dog, it will become obvious what is normal for him in terms of frequency, consistency, and color.

Healthy behavior

- Looks bright and alert
- Interacts readily with family and other pets
- Moves freely, without stiffness
- Eager to get exercise
- Not unduly tired by exercise
- Interested in food
- Drinks expected amount of water
- Urinates and defecates in normal pattern

> **"A cold wet nose** may be cited as a classic sign of health but it is **not an invariable rule."**

▽ **Perfect health**
Everything about this dog's appearance suggests normal health. He looks alert and well, in good body condition, and fit for life.

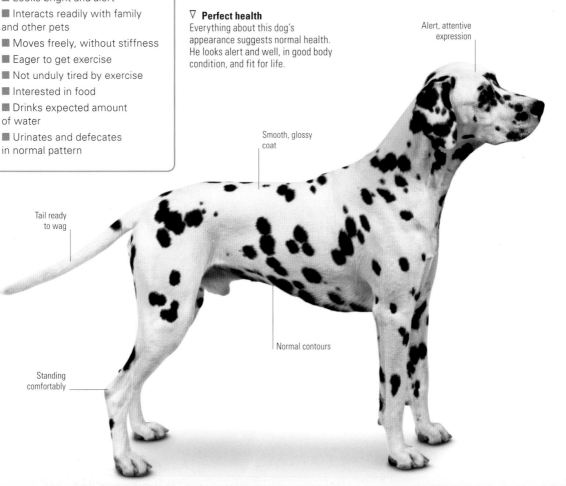

Alert, attentive expression

Smooth, glossy coat

Tail ready to wag

Normal contours

Standing comfortably

Fit to run
A dog in full health will appear bright, inquisitive, and happy. He should have a good appetite and show an obvious enjoyment of exercise.

Home checks

From early puppyhood, accustom your dog to routine checks in which you examine each part of his body. Noticing the slightest change could allow early diagnosis of a health problem, and potentially a better outcome.

While examining each part of your dog's body, talk to him to boost his confidence and use commands such as "teeth" and "ears." Look first for any obvious changes in body shape and stance, then go over him in more detail, searching for cuts, lumps, and external parasites (pp.136-7). Run your hands over and under his head and body, down all four legs, and along the length of his tail. Part the fur in places, especially over his rump; hopefully, you will find no evidence of fleas or flea dirts, there should be little or no debris, and the coat should feel and smell pleasant. Stroking your dog should be a good experience for both of you.

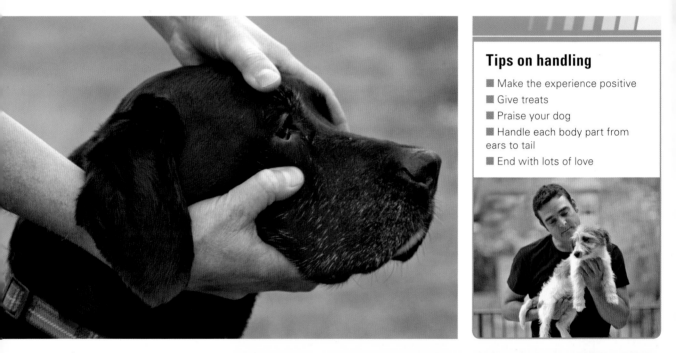

Tips on handling

■ Make the experience positive
■ Give treats
■ Praise your dog
■ Handle each body part from ears to tail
■ End with lots of love

△ *Eyes*
There should be no excessive tear production or sticky discharge. A little "sleep" is normal—simply wipe it away, using a damp cotton ball for each eye. Gently lower the bottom eyelids to check that the lining and the white around the irises are not inflamed and red.

▷ *Ears*
Your dog should not find it painful to have his ears touched. There should be no swelling of the flaps, and the ears should be clean as far down as you can see and pleasant smelling.

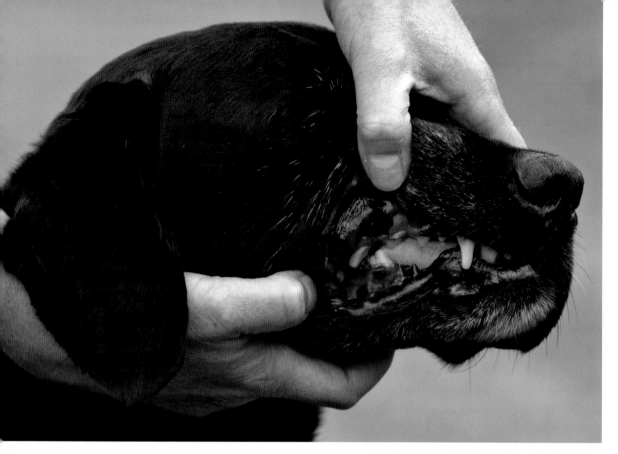

△ **Teeth**
Your dog should accept you looking in his mouth and brushing his teeth. Raise the upper lips to reveal the outer surfaces of the teeth. Ideally, these should be white, but light brown tartar may accumulate. The gums should be moist and pale pink, and the breath smell pleasant.

▽ **Paws**
Train your dog from a young age to allow his paws to be lifted up and examined. Look between the toes for irritability or sensitivity. Check for swelling and broken or overly long nails; when fully weight-bearing the nails should just touch the ground.

△ **Tail**
Look under the tail at the anus for soiling and swelling, and in a female, check the vulva for swelling and discharges. Examine the penis of a male dog for injuries and excessive discharge or bleeding from the tip.

Puppy health checks

If you have not owned a pet before, you need to find a good veterinary practice. Your choice could be based on the suggestions of friends, local advertising, or Internet searches for practices in your area.

First puppy check

Take your puppy for his first veterinary check as soon as is convenient. Unless he is already fully vaccinated, carry him into the practice, wearing a collar and lead in case he jumps out of your arms, and keep him off the floor. Alternatively, put him in a pet carrier. There are likely to be other owners with animals in the waiting room and it can be noisy, so give your puppy lots of reassurance.

Vets enjoy meeting puppies, and you are likely to receive a warm welcome. The vet will ask you for details of your puppy's early life: his date of birth; the size of the litter; how your pup compared with his littermates; where and how the pups were reared; what worming and flea treatments were carried out; and the results of any screening tests for the breed. If your puppy has been vaccinated, show the vet the certificate.

The vet will scan your puppy to see if he has been microchipped (see box, opposite), weigh him, and make a detailed examination, including checking his ears with an auroscope and listening to his heart. If a vaccination is required, it will be given now. You may need to make some follow-up appointments to complete the vaccination course and to allow the vet to monitor your puppy's progress (see p.97).

Before you leave, the vet should offer advice on diet, worm and flea control, neutering, socializing and training, and traveling in the car. Do not hesitate to ask if you need any further information.

▽ **Meeting the vet**
Your puppy should be relaxed and enjoy his first appointment at the veterinary practice. Reassure him while the vet examines him, and take the opportunity to ask any questions you may have.

"Vets enjoy meeting puppies, and you are likely to receive a **warm welcome."**

△ **Checking limbs**
The vet will examine each leg in turn, feeling along the bones and checking joint movement. This helps to detect hereditary conditions such as hip dysplasia at an early stage.

▷ **Checking ears**
Using an auroscope, the vet can make a deep examination of the ear. A common problem in puppies is infestation with ear mites, which can often be seen moving around; your vet will prescribe the appropriate treatment.

Follow-up puppy check

The veterinary practice may suggest that you take your puppy for a further checkup when he is four or five months old, to ensure that he is growing and developing well, both physically and socially. This will also give you the chance to build on the advice given at the first puppy appointment. At such a follow-up check, the vet will look for any puppy teeth that were not shed as the adult versions came through. This is important: the baby teeth may need to be removed to allow the adult teeth to grow into the right position within the mouth and ensure the correct bite.

Asking about neutering

If you plan to have your dog neutered, as the majority of owners decide to do, an early puppy health check is a good opportunity to ask for advice. Your vet will explain what the procedure involves for either a male or female and suggest

◁ **Flea combing**
A severe infestation of fleas can be serious in a young puppy. Your vet will run a fine-toothed comb through the puppy's coat to catch any live fleas or pick up flea dirt.

Microchipping

Implanting a microchip under the skin between your puppy's shoulders—a procedure much like giving a vaccination—ensures that he can always be identified. Scanning the chip reveals a unique number against which any contact information you have provided is recorded in a central database.

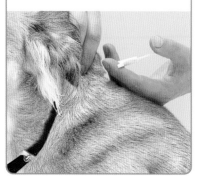

when neutering is best carried out. Veterinary opinions differ as to the ideal time for dogs to be neutered, with the recommended age ranging from a few weeks to a few months. Most commonly, the operation is performed after puberty. Many owners worry about the after-effects of neutering, and any concerns you may have can also be discussed with the vet at your puppy's health check.

Routine veterinary checks

Taking an adult dog for a regular health check is similar to taking a car for its annual service. This is when hidden problems are picked up and minor issues can be dealt with before they become major worries.

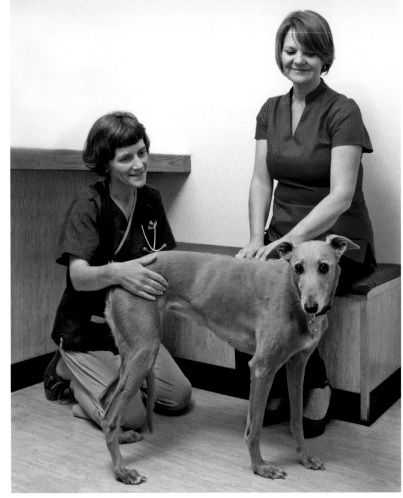

△ **Making sure all is well**
The annual checkup can be an enjoyable, social time for you, your dog, and the vet. This is your chance to discuss any concerns you may have.

▷ **Checking movement**
The vet will move your dog's joints, identifying any pain, stiffness, and reduced range of movement that may be signs of arthritis.

Annual check

If you plan to take your dog for an annual checkup, you will need to book an appointment in advance. The normal routine is for the vet to examine your dog from head to tail and ask various questions—for instance, about his thirst, appetite, diet, toileting habits, and exercise. If there is any cause for concern, detailed diagnostic tests may be recommended. You may be asked to take a sample of your dog's urine to the appointment, particularly if your pet is a senior, since this will provide additional important information about the kidneys and bladder. The sample should be collected early that morning into a suitable container (not a jar). Your vet will also be able to advise on general health matters such as weight, body and coat condition, and control of worms, fleas, and other parasites. If your dog has a microchip, it will be checked

"The normal routine is for the vet to examine your dog **from head to tail** and ask various questions. If there is any cause for concern, **diagnostic tests** may be **recommended."**

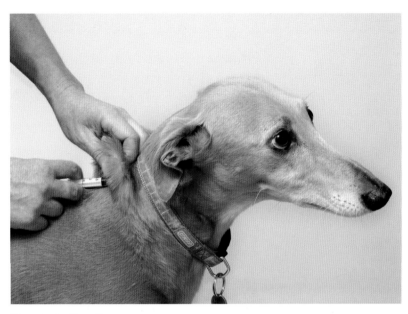

▷ **Having a vaccination**
Vaccinations give immunity against serious infectious diseases and usually require regular boosters. The vaccine is given by a relatively painless injection under the skin.

with a scanner. Other routine procedures may include clipping the nails if they are overgrown, and giving booster vaccinations to maintain protection against infectious diseases.

Some dogs do not like being examined, or resent a particular procedure, such as an ear examination. If this is the case, the vet may suggest muzzling your dog, or ask you to go out of the room and have a vet tech assist because some dogs are braver and better behaved away from their owners.

Some veterinary practices also run specific clinics, such as those dealing with dental or weight issues. These may be run by a veterinary technician, who will refer you to a veterinary surgeon if a potential problem is detected.

Dental check

A healthy mouth not only enables your dog to enjoy eating his food but is also important for his general well-being, since decayed teeth and infected gums can lead to diseases in other parts of the body. The teeth will be examined as a matter of routine at annual checks and any interim visits, but you may want to consider taking your dog to a regular dental clinic. Such clinics can give you advice on home dental hygiene techniques and will monitor your progress. They will also provide support if your dog has to undergo a dental procedure such as a clean-and-polish.

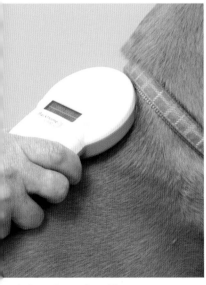

△ **Scanning a microchip**
Checking that the microchip can be identified by a scanner is very important. Remember to keep the contact information registered and the chip number up to date.

Weight clinic

If your dog's weight is recorded at a regular clinic, any changes will be identified at an early stage. Unwanted weight gain may not be readily apparent from your dog's physical appearance, so the sooner the problem is picked up, the less the dog will have to lose to return to his ideal body weight. It is equally important to pick up unintentional weight loss, which may occur in an active dog who is simply not eating enough to meet his energy requirements, but could also be warning of a health problem. Many dogs become so used to being weighed that they head straight for the scales when they come through the vet's door.

Signs of poor health

Contact your veterinarian for advice if you have any concerns about your dog, however trivial you think they might sound. If your worries prove to be unfounded then your mind will have been put at rest.

Recognizing a problem

Any change in your dog may be a warning of illness. The most trivial sign, such as a droopy eyelid, should not be dismissed because it could be significant. Your dog may have an internal problem such as a stomach upset, an external problem affecting the coat and skin, or a combination of the two. You may notice only vague signs, such as sleeping more or exercising less readily, or something obviously wrong, such as the dog limping, or shaking his head due to an ear issue.

Many common disorders are minor and easily treated, especially if they are recognized early. Always

◁ **Recognizing the warning signs**
It is helpful to understand what is normal in your dog. You will then be able to recognize anything unusual, such as lack of interest in food or exercise, that may be due to ill health.

Signs of a problem include:

- Lethargy, tiring unexpectedly on a walk
- Altered breathing pattern or an abnormal sound during respiration
- Coughing or sneezing
- Open wound
- Swelling or an unusual bump
- Blood: from a wound; passed in urine (which will appear pink or contain blood clots); in feces or vomit
- Limping or stiffness
- Unintentional weight loss
- Weight gain, particularly if the dog has developed a distended abdomen

- Reduced appetite or refusing food altogether
- Voracious appetite, or a change in what the dog will eat
- Vomiting, or regurgitation of food shortly after eating
- Diarrhea or difficulty passing a bowel movement
- Crying with pain when passing feces or urine
- Itchiness: rubbing at mouth, eyes, or ears; dragging rear along the ground ("scooting") or washing excessively at that area; or all-over bodily itching

- Abnormal discharge: from any orifice (such as the mouth, nose, ear, vulva, genitals, or anus) from which there is not usually a discharge, or because the normal smell, color, or consistency has altered
- Coat changes: dull with a greasy texture, or excessively dry; debris in the coat such as flea dirt, actual fleas, scabs, or scales
- Excessive hair loss resulting in areas of baldness
- Change in coat color (may occur so gradually that it is noticed only when compared with an old photograph)

speak to your vet before attempting any home treatment. What might seem an appropriate course of action for humans could be harmful to a dog. It may be sufficient to act on advice given by your vet practice over the telephone, although often the vet will need to examine your dog to be certain of how to proceed.

After taking a dog's history and examining him fully, the vet may still need to perform further examinations such as blood tests and imaging. Sometimes, a dog may be diagnosed with a serious disorder that needs hospitalization and even surgery, followed by a long convalescence—but, fortunately, common things really are common. An itchy dog is more likely to have fleas than an obscure problem with his nervous system.

Lifelong health

In the following pages, there is an overview of some common canine disorders, together with advice on caring for a sick dog and coping with the special problems of elderly dogs. Remember, both you and your vet are aiming for your dog to lead as long and healthy a life as possible. If you need more advice or information, your vet will be ready to help.

What is abnormal thirst?

A dog spending more time than usual at his water bowl or a source of water outside, such as a pond or bucket, may have an abnormal thirst (p.128). If he uses a bowl then measure the volume of water he drinks over a 24-hour period by emptying all his bowls and recording how much you add (in ounces); 24 hours later, measure how much is left and subtract that from the total. Divide that figure by your dog's body weight in pounds—if it is around 1.6 then your dog's thirst is normal, but contact your vet if it is 2.9 or more.

"**Any change** in your dog may be a **warning of illness**. The most **trivial sign** should **not** be **dismissed** since it could be **significant.**"

▽ **Arriving at a diagnosis**
Many common disorders, for example ear mites, are simple for a vet to diagnose, and can be easily remedied. If there is no simple explanation of a problem, your vet will work through causes in order of likelihood.

Inherited disorders

An inherited disorder is one that is handed down from one generation to the next. Such disorders appear more often in pedigree dogs and may be breed-specific. Some common examples are described below.

The risk of disease

Smaller gene pools and widespread inbreeding in the past have made pedigree dogs more likely than crossbreeds to be affected by inherited disorders. However, although crossbred dogs may be at reduced risk, they still have a chance of inheriting disease-causing genes from either parent.

Hip and elbow dysplasia

These two conditions occur mainly in medium-sized and large breeds. In dysplasia, structural defects either of the hip or the elbow cause a joint to become unstable, resulting in pain and lameness.

▷ **X-ray image of hip**
Screening is advisable before using a dog for breeding when hip dysplasia is known to occur in the breed. This involves submitting an X-ray of the dog's hips for scoring.

Hip scoring

The hips are X-rayed with the dog lying on his back, hindlegs extended straight out. For best results, the dog may need to be given sedation to keep him in the right position. Each hip joint is given a score for six factors, covering conditions from normal to severe. This gives a maximum score of 53 for each hip—the ideal is for as low a score as possible. Adding the two scores together gives a total. When selections are being made for breeding purposes, the ideal is to choose a dog whose total score is less than the current average total for that breed.

Diagnosis is based on the dog's history, together with joint manipulation and radiology.

Treatment may consist of pain relief, reduced exercise, and maintaining ideal body weight. Various surgical options are also available, including total hip replacement for hip dysplasia. After a certain age (generally more than one year old) susceptible breeds can be screened for hip and elbow dysplasia.

Aortic stenosis

A congenital defect, present from birth, aortic stenosis is a narrowing of the aortic valve in the heart.

There may be no signs, the disorder being detected as a murmur when a vet listens to the heart with a stethoscope at a puppy check. It may be investigated further (with X-ray, ultrasound, and ECG) or simply monitored, since only a few dogs can be treated surgically. Some dogs with aortic stenosis go on to develop congestive heart failure.

Blood clotting disorders

The most common inherited clotting disorder (in both dogs and humans) is hemophilia, in which lack of an essential factor for blood clotting results in recurrent

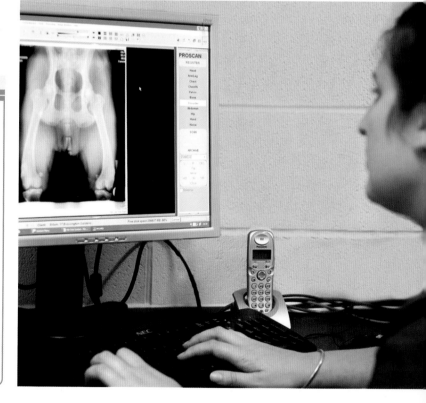

◁ **German Shorthaired Pointer**
Many breeds, including the German Shorthaired Pointer, can be affected by Von Willebrand's disease, an inherited blood clotting disorder.

▽ **Collie eye anomaly (CEA)**
Collies such as the Australian Shepherd must be checked as puppies for CEA, because early signs can be masked as the dog matures.

> "**Screening** is important. The **advent** of **DNA** screening has **improved** the chances of **detecting** many **inherited diseases.**"

bleeding. The faulty gene responsible is passed on by affected males to their female offspring, who remain unaffected themselves but can be carriers of the gene. Hemophilia occurs in both pedigree and crossbred dogs.

A similar inherited bleeding disorder is Von Willebrand's disease, which can affect either sex. Many breeds can be affected, including Dobermans and German Shepherds; DNA tests are available for some breeds.

Eye problems
Dogs can be affected by several inherited eye conditions, including some that are easily visible, such as entropion (p.112), and others that need internal examination of the eye using specialized equipment. An eye disease that can occur in any breed and also in crossbred dogs is progressive retinal atrophy (PRA). In this disorder, there is degeneration of the retina—the layer of light-sensitive cells at the back of the eye—leading to loss of vision. An owner may become aware of PRA only when a dog has difficulties in seeing, which at first may be only at night.

PRA is diagnosed from examining the retina with an ophthalmoscope, and the vet may recommend more specialized examinations. There is no treatment, and loss of vision is permanent. DNA screening is available for some breeds.

Breeds of collies (Rough, Smooth, and Border Collies, Shetland Sheepdogs, and Australian Shepherds) and some other breeds are affected by a disorder known as collie eye anomaly (CEA), in which there are abnormalities in the choroid, a layer of tissue at the back of the eye. CEA can be detected from birth, so pups are examined before they are three months old. The mildest form of CEA has little effect on sight, but the most severe form can cause blindness. DNA screening is available.

Screening for disease
Routine screening is important in reducing the incidence of inherited diseases. For hip and elbow dysplasia, dogs are screened by having X-rays taken (see box, left). Eye conditions such as PRA and CEA once relied on examination and certification; however, the advent of DNA screening has improved the chances of detecting both these and many other inherited diseases.

Musculoskeletal disorders

Just like us, dogs are susceptible to minor strains and sprains, which usually resolve with rest. Sometimes a problem is more serious, so seek veterinary help if your dog persistently limps or is unwilling to exercise.

Signs of a problem

- Limping (head lifted as lame forelimb lands on ground)
- Stiffness after resting
- Unwillingness to exercise; hanging back while on walk
- Reluctance to climb stairs or to jump into car
- Pain, swelling, and heat in joint
- Ataxia (loss of coordination) and paralysis
- Sudden halt durning activity (and perhaps holding up back paw)

Arthritis

If a joint is unstable due to an injury or to a skeletal abnormality such as hip dysplasia, arthritis may develop as a dog ages. This disease is associated with damage and inflammation that restrict joint movement and cause pain. Normal wear and tear can also lead to arthritis, especially if a dog has led a very active life or is overweight.

To investigate and diagnose an arthritic joint, your vet will palpate and manipulate the area, looking for swelling, heat, and abnormal movement, and may want to watch your dog move as you walk him. Further investigation may be needed, such as X-rays or withdrawal of a small sample of fluid from the joint for testing. MRI scanning is also increasingly used.

As well as pain relief with non-steroidal anti-inflammatory drugs, other ways of managing arthritis include weight control,

△ **Elderly but active**
It is important to keep your senior dog's limbs moving, but he is likely to enjoy two or three short daily walks more than one tiring, long hike.

changing your dog's exercise regime (taking him for more frequent but shorter walks), acupuncture, non-weight-bearing exercise such as swimming (hydrotherapy), and physiotherapy. Glucosamine, chondroitin, hyaluronic acid, and omega-3 fatty acids may also help, either taken as dietary supplements or included within the formulation of certain foods.

Panosteitis

In young, still-developing dogs, a bone disease called panosteitis can affect bone growth, causing lameness in different limbs at different times. This condition is especially common in larger breeds such as German Shepherds and

△ Problems with stairs
If your dog has back pain, the prospect of going up a flight of stairs can be as daunting to him as climbing a mountain.

Labrador Retrievers. Panosteitis is confirmed by X-ray and treated with rest and pain relief. The problem is usually temporary.

Prolapsed disc

A dog who is suddenly reluctant to go up stairs or jump into the car may have temporary neck or back pain, which improves with rest and anti-inflammatory drugs. A more serious problem, seen especially in long-backed breeds such as Bassett Hounds and Dachshunds, is prolapse of one or more intervertebral discs. Symptoms may include pain, weakness, or paralysis of the hindlimbs—and the forelimbs if the prolapse is in the neck—and loss of sensation below the area of the affected disc. Strict rest and pain relief may be enough for recovery, but surgery, after X-ray and MRI to pinpoint the problem, may be needed. If bladder and bowel control are lost, the outlook is poor.

Hindleg disorders

It is common to see a dog, particularly a small breed such as a West Highland White or Yorkshire Terrier, trotting along and then skipping while carrying one backleg off the ground for a few steps before walking on all four paws again. He probably has an intermittently slipping kneecap (luxating patella), commonly caused by the groove housing the kneecap being too shallow. The problem can be corrected surgically, but this is usually only necessary in a big dog, since little dogs cope very well.

Another common hindleg problem is rupture of the cranial cruciate ligament, one of the stabilizing ligaments within the knee joint. This is often associated with an active dog who dashes off after a ball only to stop suddenly, holding up a back paw. Golden Retrievers and German Shepherds are among the breeds that seem to be prone. Surgery offers the best chance of recovery. For small dogs, pain relief and strict rest for several weeks may work.

△ Restricted exercise
If your dog's exercise must be restricted after a joint injury, keep him on a lead to prevent possibly harmful bursts of overactivity.

Avoiding overload

Keeping your dog's weight at the correct level for his size and breed is one of the most important things you can do to help prevent joint problems. Obesity is not only detrimental to your dog's general health, it also overloads his joints, increasing the risk of irreversible and painful disorders such as arthritis.

Coat and skin disorders

A dog's coat and skin are easy to see, so problems with them are very common reasons for a trip to the vet. Do not ignore constant scratching or licking, which can turn a minor disorder into something more serious.

Signs of a problem

- Dull, greasy coat
- Scale, scabs, and crusts on skin or in coat
- Skin rash or spots
- Hair loss
- Change in color of skin or hair
- Itchiness
- Unpleasant odor
- Excessive licking or scratching
- Unexplained bumps or lumps

Allergy and infection

Dogs that are allergic to fleas, substances such as pollen, or certain foods often react with itchiness. Skin allergies, especially if they cause constant scratching, can lead to recurrent skin infections needing repeated, long cycles of antibiotics. It is important to try to identify the triggers of an allergy, because it may be possible to avoid the problem (by changing to a hypoallergenic diet, for example), or to treat it with a medication or desensitizing vaccine. Antihistamines can help limit itchiness, but some dogs need low-dose corticosteroids.

Acute moist dermatitis

Also known as a hot spot, this is a sticky area of infected, oozy, often smelly skin that the dog exacerbates by repeatedly licking and scratching. The original cause may have been an insect sting. Treatment is aimed at thoroughly cleansing the area and preventing further self-harm, together with antibiotics and bathing twice daily with a teaspoonful of salt in half a quart of warm water.

Anal furunculosis

If your dog shows extreme pain when eliminating, he may have a serious, deep-seated condition in the tissues around the anus known as anal furunculosis. The disorder may be accompanied by colitis or irritable bowel syndrome. Looking under the tail reveals a raw, foul-smelling area of ulceration. The current approach is drug treatment to suppress the immune response that causes the problem, with surgery if the area does not heal fully. However, unfortunately treatment is not always successful.

△ **Itchy skin**
Fleas are the most common cause of skin irritation, but if fine-combing fails to detect them, ask your vet to check your dog for other possible problems.

Sebaceous adenitis

This autoimmune disorder targets the hair follicles, especially the glands within them that produce sebum, the oily substance that protects and waterproofs the hair and skin. Symptoms include alopecia (hair loss), scaling of the skin, and sometimes intense itching. Recurrent secondary bacterial skin infections can be a complication. Treatment relies on shampoos, oil baths, dietary supplements, and antibiotics.

Ringworm

A highly contagious fungal skin infection, ringworm can be transmitted to humans. The disease causes scaling and crusting of the skin, and hair loss. It is usually diagnosed by checking the area with a fluorescent lamp or placing hairs on a culture medium and watching for signs of fungal growth. Other pets should be tested as well. Treatment includes shampoos, creams, and oral drugs. The fungal spores can persist for months, so you should destroy all your dog's grooming tools, collars, leads, and bedding, and vigorously vacuum your house and car.

Skin growths

Growths such as cysts, warts, and tumors may be seen or felt in your dog's skin. Always have lumps investigated—early diagnosis and treatment could be vital. Your vet may take a few cells or a small section of the mass for diagnosis before making a plan for action.

Persistent licking
Allowing a dog to lick at an itchy area, perhaps after an insect sting, can lead to infection and a worse problem to manage. On the lower leg, covering the area with a sock may be enough to break the cycle.

Eye disorders

Always check that your dog's eyes are open and bright. Many eye problems quickly become obvious, but some disorders affecting the inside of the eye may not be suspected until the dog's sight is affected.

Signs of a problem

- Eyelids fully or partially closed
- Watery discharge
- Sticky, yellow-green discharge
- Pawing at eyes
- Increased blink rate
- Reduced vision, bumping into objects
- Red eye
- Swollen eye or eyelids

Conjunctivitis

Unlike the highly infectious eye disorder that affects people, conjunctivitis in dogs simply means inflammation of the conjunctiva, the layer covering the front of the eyeball. The most apparent sign is reddening inside the lower eyelid. There may be a discharge, initially clear but becoming white or green if an infection develops. Your dog may blink rapidly because of pain. The inflammation is sometimes due to an allergy to pollen, but the most common causes of conjunctivitis in one eye are foreign bodies, such as a grass awn or a speck of dirt or sand.

Your vet may numb the front of the eye with local anesthetic drops to make an examination. Fluorescein dye applied to the eye may reveal an injury to the cornea such as a scratch. There may be a film over the eye due to an inflamed cornea, as well as conjunctivitis. Prompt attention is needed as the iris can be affected too, with painful spasm of the pupil. Your dog may be prescribed pain relief and oral antibiotics as well as eye drops, and will need careful monitoring. For allergy-related conjunctivitis, steroid eye drops help to reduce inflammation. Your dog may need an Elizabethan collar to stop him from rubbing his eye.

Entropion and ectropion

The eyelids have a protective role but if they roll inward, a condition called entropion, the eyelashes rub against the front of the eye causing conjunctivitis and corneal ulceration. Entropion is usually congenital, but can develop after injury or as a result of chronic conjunctivitis. The dog will blink more often and rub at his eyes, resulting in infection and a thick discharge. Entropion is corrected by surgery, although there is a risk of overcorrection and ectropion, an

◁ **Vet check**
Eye problems need prompt attention from a vet. Do not ignore signs such as a discharge or a dog pawing at his eyes because of irritation.

◁ **Eye problems in the Shar Pei**
Entropion, a painful inrolling of the eyelids, is common in the Shar Pei, usually developing in very young puppies. Both upper and lower eyelids may be affected.

outward rolling of the eyelid that exposes the eye to potential injury. Ectropion can also occur naturally, congenitally, or in old age. Usually, only extreme cases are corrected. Some breeds, such as the English Bulldog and Cocker Spaniel, are prone to a combination of entropion and ectropion.

Cataract
In this disorder, the transparent lens of the eye, which directs light to the retina, becomes opaque, impairing sight. Cataracts can be hereditary or may form in response to retinal disease, glaucoma, or diabetes (p.132). Senile cataracts may develop in old dogs. Cataracts can be removed surgically, usually only if the retina is intact so that the dog can see afterward.

Glaucoma
Raised pressure within the eyeball, known as glaucoma, causes pain and ultimately loss of vision. The condition can be treated but needs early diagnosis to avoid blindness. Glaucoma is an inherited problem in some breeds, including Beagles and Bassett Hounds.

Dry eye
Lack of tear production to lubricate the eyes results in dryness and a thick discharge due to infection. Dry eye is diagnosed by a painless test and treated with eye drops or surgery. It is an inherited problem in some breeds, for example, the West Highland White Terrier.

Horner's syndrome
This set of symptoms usually affects one eye only, with a sunken eyeball, drooping of the upper eyelid, prominence of the third eyelid at the inner corner of the eye, and constriction of the pupil. The cause is often unknown and it resolves itself, but your dog should be examined by a vet for possible underlying health problems.

Applying eye drops

Supporting your dog's head, gently pull down on the lower eyelid and raise the upper lid.

Hold the dropper between your thumb and forefinger and squeeze the drops onto the front of the eye.

After applying the drops, gently hold your dog's eyelids closed for a few seconds.

Ear disorders

The most common ear problems in dogs are infections, mites, and foreign bodies in the ear canal; some breeds are prone to deafness. See your vet promptly if your dog is showing any signs of an ear problem.

Signs of a problem

- ■ Shaking head, yelping
- ■ Rubbing at one ear
- ■ Rubbing at both ears (can be sign of an allergy)
- ■ Smelly ear or ears
- ■ Pain when ear is touched
- ■ Pain while eating
- ■ Deafness
- ■ Swollen ear flap (aural hematoma)
- ■ Head tilt, loss of balance, nausea (can be signs of middle or inner ear disease)

Aural hematoma

Bleeding can sometimes occur inside a dog's ear flap, causing a swelling known as an aural hematoma. This condition may occur in a dog that constantly flicks his head about or scratches his ear. Often, the hematoma is accompanied by infection in the outer ear canal. A vet may be able to reduce the swelling by draining the blood through a needle and injecting a corticosteroid. Some dogs can tolerate this procedure without sedation. Surgery is also an option. Left untreated, the ear flap will shrink and crinkle.

Outer ear problems

If you see your dog rubbing at his ear, he may be troubled by an allergy, ear mites, or an infection. Another common problem is a sharp grass awn lodged in the outer ear canal; this is extremely painful and your dog will probably react by vigorously shaking his head and yelping.

To look down the full length of the outer canal to the ear drum, your vet will use a viewing instrument called an auroscope. This examination can be painful for your dog and he may have to be sedated first.

◁ **Hazard in the grass**
A dog that suddenly starts pawing at an ear, shaking his head, and squealing after running outdoors is likely to have picked up a grass awn in the outer ear canal. Removal may have to be done under sedation or general anesthetic.

▽ **Binding an ear**
A cut ear flap will bleed profusely from even a small nick. The wound should be treated and the ear bandaged to the head to prevent the dog from flicking it and causing fresh bleeding.

Ear mites are treated with ear drops or topical products that are applied directly to the skin on the back of the neck. Infections are initially treated with antibiotic ear drops, but if this fails, the vet will take a swab for microscopic examination and testing for drug sensitivity. The infected ear may be flushed under general anesthetic; occasionally, surgery is necessary. Grass awns may be removed under general anesthetic.

Middle and inner ear

Infections of the outer ear sometimes spread to the middle part of the ear. Another cause of middle ear infection is penetration of the eardrum by a foreign body. Middle and inner ear infections can also be caused by an adverse reaction to ear drops used to treat outer ear problems. The signs of infection include pain on opening

▷ **Avoid water**
Try to prevent your dog from swimming if he is prone to ear infections. Exercise him away from water if the temptation to jump in is too great.

the mouth, lethargy, and discharge. Other common signs are loss of balance, head tilting, and vomiting.

In both middle and inner ear disease, early diagnosis—often with imaging such as radiography and MRI—and treatment are vital.

Deafness

Many older dogs are affected by age-related deafness and are hard to wake or fail to come when you call—but you should suspect selective deafness if your senior reacts promptly to the rattle of a food bowl. Congenital deafness is

often hereditary and possibly linked to coat color; white-coated breeds, such as the English Bull Terrier and the Dalmatian, are particularly susceptible. A profoundly deaf puppy can be identified readily, since he responds to sounds differently from the rest of his litter.

Your dog's hearing can be assessed using the Brainstem Auditory Evoked Response test (BAER) which detects electrical activity in the inner ear and aural pathways of the brain. It is painless and can be performed on puppies without distressing them, although older dogs may need sedation.

"In **middle** and **inner ear** disease, **early diagnosis** and **treatment** are **vital**."

Applying ear drops

Shake the bottle if the ear drops are in suspension, and gently pull back the ear flap to expose the ear canal.

Still holding back the ear flap, squirt the recommended number of drops into the ear canal.

Gently massage the ear to help the drops to penetrate. Afterward, give your dog plenty of praise and a treat.

Mouth and tooth disorders

We should look after our dogs' teeth and gums just as we do our own, to minimize the chances of disease. Regular dental checks, which can be carried out at a veterinary practice, are important to a dog's health.

Signs of a problem

- Bad breath (halitosis)
- Discoloration of teeth
- Yellow deposit of calcified plaque on teeth
- Swelling on side of face (tooth root abscess)
- Gray discharge at gumline (pus from tooth root abscess)
- Difficulty eating, perhaps yelping with pain (rotten or broken tooth, something stuck across roof of mouth or between the teeth)
- Drooling saliva, pus, or blood
- Gum proliferation or growth

Plaque and hygiene

In a healthy mouth, a dog's teeth are white and his gums a pale pink. Ideally, the teeth should be brushed regularly at home to remove plaque, a soft colorless substance that accumulates on the teeth after eating. With time, plaque hardens as yellow tartar or calculus, which needs to be removed with an ultrasonic scaler under general anesthetic.

Without intervention, plaque buildup can lead to gum disease, and teeth may ultimately loosen and fall out. If infection sets in, you may see pus at the gumline, or a swelling on the cheek caused by a tooth root abscess. Your dog may have smelly breath or drool blood-tinged saliva; he may have trouble eating, perhaps pawing at his mouth because of pain and refusing hard treats and dried foods. If your dog's mouth is very painful, he may have to be anesthetized for the vet to find out exactly what is going on.

Teeth that cannot be saved will be extracted. Advanced dental procedures such as root canal treatment may be possible. After extractions, your dog will be

▽ **Dental check-up**
Your vet will look at your dog's teeth and mouth as part of a general examination, and may recommend that you book a dental clinic appointment for a more specific check.

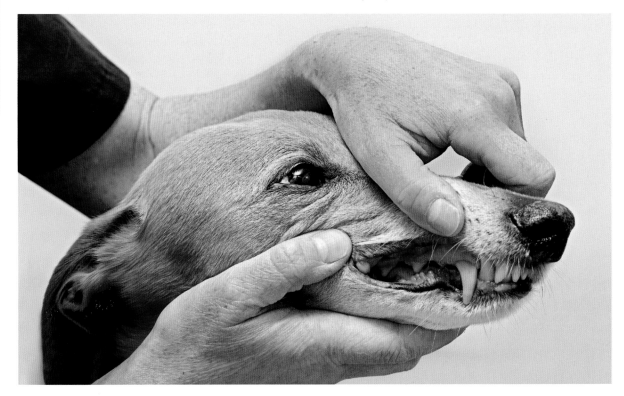

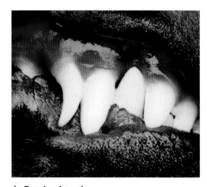

△ **Retained teeth**
Here, the puppy upper canine can be seen sitting behind (to the left), of the adult tooth, causing a potential food trap.

▷ **Underbite jaw**
The lower jaw jutting out in front of the upper jaw is a feature of some breeds, such as this Bulldog, contributing to the shape of the face.

discharged with antibiotics and pain relief. Because plaque starts accumulating as soon as your dog starts eating again, vigilant home care is vital, together with regular dental checkups.

Retained puppy teeth

Sometimes the puppy teeth do not fall out when the adult versions break through. Having both sets can crowd the other teeth and create food traps, leading to infection. Your vet will probably recommend removal of any unwanted puppy teeth (most conveniently, this could be done when your puppy is anesthetized to be neutered).

Malocclusions

If a dog's jaws are not aligned correctly, the teeth do not rest against each other normally, which is described as a malocclusion or, more commonly, an overbite or underbite. This can be a recognized feature of some breeds, but is regarded as a fault in others. Malocclusion carries an increased risk of periodontal disease (that is, in the tissues surrounding the teeth) so careful dental hygiene, including tooth brushing, is very important. Your vet will look for misaligned teeth at your puppy's first check. Malocclusion can occasionally occur after an accident such as a fall onto the face.

Foreign objects

Pieces of wood, chews, and bones can all become wedged across the roof of the mouth or between teeth. Sedation or general anesthesia may be needed to examine the mouth, remove the foreign object, and treat any injuries caused.

Jaw drop

This curious condition is characterized by a sudden inability to close the mouth, together with excessive salivation and difficulty swallowing. Despite appearances, it is not painful. Fortunately, jaw drop usually cures itself over several days; the main concern is to ensure that your dog gets enough food and water.

Jaw pain

Inflammation can sometimes develop in the muscles used for chewing, making it painful for a dog to eat. The dog may not be able to close his mouth fully and will drool saliva, looking as though he might have jaw drop. Jaw pain is seen in all breeds but especially in German Shepherds. The condition usually responds to a course of high-dose corticosteroids.

Care after dental treatment

When you collect your dog from the vet after a dental procedure, he may be drooling, which is common after a general anesthetic. Let him settle at home before you feed him. Unless he was discharged with a prescription diet, offer a small amount of bland home-cooked food such as chicken and rice. Continue with this for a few days, especially if he had extractions, weaning him back to his usual diet once his mouth has healed.

Respiratory disorders

It is easy to spot if your dog has a respiratory problem. Normally, a dog breathes through his mouth and pants only when he is hot or after exertion. If the pattern changes, or he develops a cough, consult your vet.

Signs of a problem

■ Nasal discharge (on one or both sides—watery, white-green, or bloody)

■ Sneezing or honking (reverse sneezing)

■ Painful, one-sided facial swelling, which may affect the eye on that side

■ Noisy breathing

■ Difficulty breathing, with increased chest movements

■ Poor exercise tolerance

■ Cough

■ Bluish tinge to gums (indicating shortage of oxygen in blood, due to reduced lung function)

△ **Close contact**
Airborne infections spread rapidly between dogs housed in close proximity, either in kennels or within a household.

Inhaled foreign body

Sniffing is what dogs do, and if they inhale an object, they usually expel it by sneezing. However, something like a grass awn in a nostril can be on a one-way journey. Despite paroxysms of sneezing, the awn may move through the nasal chamber, scratching the delicate lining. The first sign of trouble may be a discharge, initially colorless but becoming thick and white or green as bacteria move in. It is therefore important to remove the awn as soon as possible. The vet may be able to see a foreign body through an auroscope inserted into the nostril; otherwise, under general anesthetic, the object may be located through a fine endoscope passed down the dog's nose, and then removed.

Kennel cough

This highly contagious disorder is usually a viral infection, although it can also be caused by *Bordetella bronchiseptica,* a common secondary bacterial invader. Kennel cough spreads readily between dogs, especially if they are housed together, such as in kennels and at dog shows; animals in a multi-dog household are also vulnerable.

The dog may seem well, apart from coughing up white frothy sputum, or he may be lethargic with a fever. For viral infections, treatment is aimed at relieving illness and the dog should be isolated until coughing stops, to prevent the spread of infection. Antibiotics are used only for bacterial infections.

Honking

In some dogs the soft palate (the flexible tissue at the back of the mouth) is longer than normal, which can result in it being inhaled into the airway. When this happens, the dog makes a characteristic honking sound as he tries to catch his breath until the airway clears. Excitement and exertion are common triggers, as is an allergic reaction to pollen. Corrective surgery may be needed if honking is a persistent problem.

Laryngeal paralysis

This disorder of the larynx (voice box) occurs from middle age onward in any type of dog but often in Labradors and Golden Retrievers. There is noisy breathing, often with a hoarse

▽ **Voice box problems**
In laryngeal paralysis, the vocal cords in the larynx (or voice box) do not function properly. The disorder is most commonly seen in large breeds such as the Golden Retriever.

cough, an altered bark, reduced ability to exercise, and sometimes severe difficulty breathing. Laryngeal paralysis can develop for no apparent reason, but may occur if a neck or chest injury causes damage to the nerves controlling the larynx, and is sometimes an effect of an underactive thyroid.

Any underlying cause should be treated if possible. Corticosteroids can sometimes improve the problem. Surgery to reduce breathing difficulties is high risk.

Lung disorders

Diseases of the lungs can include bronchitis (especially in older dogs), pneumonia, tumors, and fluid buildup due to heart failure.

Such problems restrict lung function, causing the dog to breathe more rapidly and noisily and/or develop a cough. X-rays are often used to diagnose lung disorders and can sometimes be carried out without sedation, an important factor if a dog is having difficulty breathing. If it is necessary to examine the airway directly, for example if a trapped foreign body is suspected, then an endoscope may be passed down under general anesthetic.

Many lung disorders respond to drug treatment. It may be possible to surgically remove a single lung tumor, but multiple secondary growths, usually a sign of advanced cancer, are likely to be inoperable.

Preventing the spread of respiratory disease

The spread of diseases passed on by infected droplets can be prevented by quickly isolating a dog who is coughing or is known to have been in contact with a coughing dog. Vaccination may provide some protection against kennel cough, depending on the specific bacteria or virus.

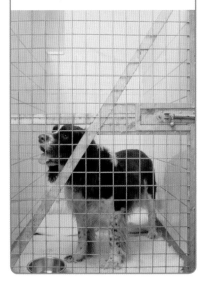

Heart and blood disorders

A healthy heart and circulation are essential to life. If a dog has a heart or blood disorder, early diagnosis is vital. Treatment should include good home management and regular monitoring; surgery may be an option.

Signs of a problem

- Cough
- Labored breathing
- Blue (cyanotic) gums and tongue
- Fatigue and lethargy
- Poor exercise tolerance, tires easily
- Weight loss
- Reduced appetite and increased thirst
- Bloated abdomen
- Fainting (syncope)
- In anemia: pale gums, or yellowing of gums and whites of eyes, fatigue, black feces, blood in urine.

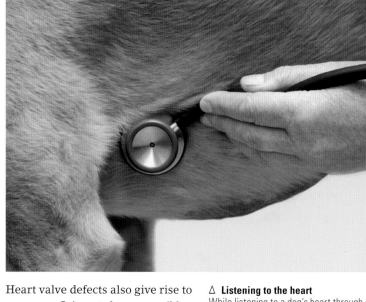

Congenital heart defect

Sometimes a puppy's heart does not develop normally in the womb, leading to congenital defects (present from birth). One of the most common of such disorders is called patent ductus arteriosus (PDA). Before a puppy is born, its blood bypasses the lungs through a channel (called the ductus arteriosus) running between the pulmonary artery and the aorta. In PDA, the channel does not close as it should soon after birth, and normal circulation is disrupted. The defect is heard through a stethoscope as a murmur, or blurring of the clear "lub-dub" sounds of a normal heartbeat. PDA is confirmed with radiography, ultrasound scanning, and ECG; in most cases the problem can be surgically corrected.

Heart valve defects also give rise to murmurs. It is not always possible to correct such defects surgically, and congestive heart failure (below) may develop later.

Congestive heart failure

In this disorder, the heart fails to pump efficiently. A common cause of congestive heart failure in old dogs is a diseased heart valve. Your vet may detect a murmur before a problem becomes apparent, and might not happen in your dog's lifetime. Early signs of congestive heart failure are typically a reduced ability to exercise, with panting and breathlessness. In the later stages, a cough develops, often at night and early in the morning, and the dog loses weight and has a reduced appetite but an increased thirst.

△ **Listening to the heart**
While listening to a dog's heart through a stethoscope, the vet will pick up any abnormal sounds that could indicate a problem.

His abdomen may swell with fluid, making him look pot-bellied. Diagnostic tests for congestive heart failure include ultrasound scan, X-rays, ECG, and blood tests. Treatment includes drugs, a prescription diet, and weight management, and surgery for an underlying cause may be possible.

Dilated cardiomyopathy

This condition especially affects Boxers, Dobermans, and Great Danes. The heart is unable to contract properly and there may be a disordered heart rhythm, resulting in weakness, difficulty breathing, a cough, fainting, loss of appetite, and weight loss.

X-rays, ultrasound scan, and ECG confirm the diagnosis. Treatment is aimed at improving quality of life, since the outlook is, sadly, poor.

Blood abnormalities

Dogs can be affected by various blood disorders, one of the most common of which is anemia. In this condition, the blood has a reduced oxygen-carrying capacity because of either insufficient red blood cells or a low concentration of the oxygen-carrying pigment hemoglobin. Types of anemia include an immune system disorder called immune-mediated hemolytic anemia (p.135), and iron-deficiency anemia, which could be caused, for example, by bleeding from a stomach ulcer, and is indicated by a dog passing dark feces. Treatment of anemia depends on the underlying cause.

Clotting disorders are often inherited (pp.104–5), but can be an effect of eating rat poison (p.163).

Home care for your dog

The key to caring for a dog with a heart condition is to let him take life at his own pace, avoiding undue stress—which may mean leading a quieter life yourself. Exercise should be short and gentle, perhaps in the yard, so that he can stop and rest when he wants. He will need to avoid weight gain, which will put additional stress on his heart. Your vet may recommend a specific prescription diet for dogs with heart disease.

△ **Breed at risk**
The Great Dane is a breed prone to dilated cardiomyopathy. Early diagnosis is important so that drug treatment can be started before the disease has become too advanced.

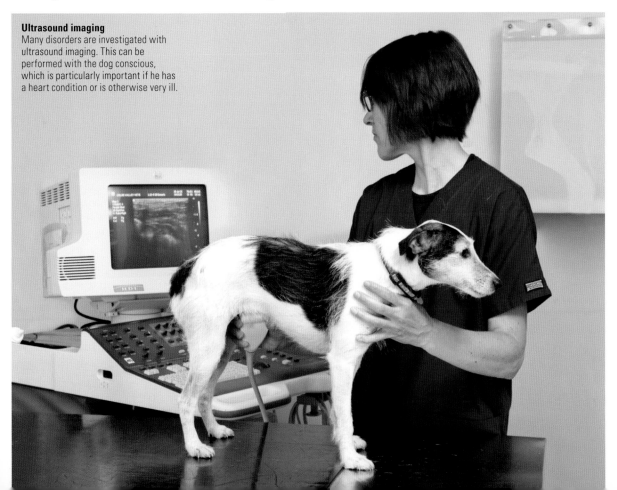

Ultrasound imaging
Many disorders are investigated with ultrasound imaging. This can be performed with the dog conscious, which is particularly important if he has a heart condition or is otherwise very ill.

Digestive disorders

Minor stomach upsets are common in dogs, who are always ready to grab forbidden food. Having a good gag reflex, they usually vomit up anything unsuitable. Occasionally, more serious gastric problems can arise.

Signs of a problem:

- Vomiting or regurgitation
- Constipation (as a result of, for example, eating bones)
- Diarrhea (frequently passing large volumes of loose feces)
- Colitis (straining to pass loose feces containing mucus and blood)
- Altered stools (either in color, frequency, or consistency)
- Weight loss

Obstruction

A brief bout of vomiting usually means a short-lived stomach upset. Repeated vomiting may indicate a foreign body, such as a bone or a child's toy, blocking the stomach or intestine. If the object is in the stomach, the dog can appear quite normal; a dog with an intestinal obstruction looks uncomfortable, standing crouched over a painful abdomen. This condition needs rapid investigation. A small foreign object may be retrieved from the stomach via an endoscope passed down the throat. Otherwise, surgery is needed. During recovery, the dog needs light food, such as chicken with boiled rice.

Obstruction due to "bloat" is a medical and surgical emergency. In this condition, gas accumulates in the stomach causing bloating (gastric dilatation) and sometimes twisting of the stomach (volvulus). Large deep-chested breeds like the Great Dane are particularly prone to this disorder. Your dog should be seen by a vet as soon as possible if he is restless, retching, and drooling, especially after eating, and has a distended abdomen. To help avoid bloat, your dog should rest, and avoid drinking much water for an hour before or after eating. Feeding several small meals throughout the day also helps ease the symptoms.

Constipation is another form of obstruction, which may cause a dog to lose his appetite and even vomit. Treatment depends on the underlying cause (for example, eating bones) and the severity of the constipation. If laxatives are ineffective, an enema will be given under general anesthetic.

Diarrhea

Sudden change in diet is a very common cause of diarrhea in dogs. Introduce any new food to your dog by mixing it with his usual meals in

◁ **Risk of obstruction**
If your dog swallows a large object such as a piece of wood or a stone, or even something unusual like a sock or child's toy, it may lodge in the stomach or intestines, causing vomiting.

△ **Taking time to recover**
Your dog will feel lethargic and sleep more than usual while recovering from a stomach upset. Encourage him to drink frequent small amounts of rehydration fluid or cool bottled water and avoid strenuous exercise until he is well.

▽ **Light meals**
When a dog is recovering from a digestive disorder, he needs small frequent meals once he can keep fluids down. Your vet may put him on a prescription diet, but otherwise offer him easily digested food, such as chicken.

ever-increasing proportions, giving the natural gut flora time to adjust.

Most adult dogs are lactose intolerant and will have diarrhea if they drink cows' milk. Less common is intolerance to gluten, the protein found in wheat, which also causes diarrhea and weight loss. Blood tests and diarrhea clearing up on a trial gluten-free diet confirm the diagnosis.

Pancreatic problems
The pancreas produces important digestive enzymes, but if it fails to produce enough the result will be a ravenous dog with diarrhea and weight loss. Pancreatic function is checked by blood tests, and missing enzymes will be replaced with dietary supplements.

A more serious illness is inflammation of the pancreas (pancreatitis). A high-fat meal is a common trigger, such as eating

suet left out for wild birds. Symptoms may be vague but can include intermittent vomiting and acute abdominal pain and swelling. Blood tests and an ultrasound scan confirm the diagnosis. Treatment includes pain relief, anti-nausea medication, and hospitalization for intravenous fluid therapy.

Dangers of dehydration
Small dogs and puppies in particular can become dehydrated and weak from recurrent vomiting and diarrhea (gastroenteritis) within a matter of hours and, at worst, may need to be hospitalized and given fluids intravenously. If you are at all concerned about a dog or puppy with gastroenteritis, contact your vet as early as possible.

Reproductive disorders

Various problems can affect the reproductive organs of dogs, including infections and tumors. Neutering, which is often advised in the case of family pets, can reduce the risk of serious disorders in both sexes.

Signs of a problem

- Distended abdomen (in female)
- Discharge from vulva
- Enlargement of mammary glands and milk production
- Lumps in mammary glands
- Behavioral changes (in female)
- Irregularly sized testicles

Normal cycles in females

If you have an unneutered female, it is important to understand what happens during her normal reproductive cycle. A dog can be expected to have her first menses from six months of age, and she will then continue to come into heat every 6–12 months, although there can be wide variations. She will lose a variable quantity of blood from the vulva, which you may miss if she is meticulous about washing. If you do not want her to be mated, you should isolate her while she is in heat to avoid attracting every intact male in the area.

False pregnancy

This is a normal part of the female's reproductive cycle that happens a few weeks after her cycle is over. Often, a female shows signs of maternal behavior, or nesting, when she takes toys and other objects into her bed. Her teats may become swollen and her mammary glands may start producing milk. False pregnancy can, however, also result in unpredictable behavior and aggression, which may respond to drug treatment.

Mammary tumors

Tumors of the mammary glands often develop around the time a female is in heat, with the influx of hormones, but they can also arise independently of the reproductive cycle. Mammary tumors may be benign but if they are malignant, they have the potential to spread to adjacent mammary glands and to the lungs. The likelihood of tumors developing is reduced by neutering before your female has had many

◁ **Taking an interest**
In a sexually mature dog, taking an interest in the opposite sex is natural. Neutering not only prevents unwanted behavior but can lessen the risk of many reproductive disorders.

△ **Nesting instinct**
It is quite normal for an unneutered female to experience regular false pregnancies. She may treat her bed as a nest, collecting up objects as though to mother them, and may sometimes become quite possessive about them.

cycles. Your vet will routinely run a hand along your female's belly, feeling the mammary glands for masses. Should you find a growth then contact your vet.

Womb infection

Infection of the womb, or pyometra, classically develops a few weeks after a dog has been in heat. You may notice that there is an unpleasant discharge from her vulva but little other apparent illness. Alternatively, your dog may be very ill, running a fever, lacking an appetite, vomiting, drinking excessively and urinating frequently. She may have a tender, distended abdomen. The usual treatment is neutering, but the risk of complications is high because of the dog being unwell. Sometimes the infection clears up with a course of antibiotics but is likely to return after the next cycle. Ideally, neutering can take place before then, while the dog is fit and healthy.

Retained testicles

In male dogs, one testicle or both may be retained within the abdomen or in the groin rather than being in the scrotum. If a puppy has retained testicles, the vet will regularly check the scrotum until the testicles are fully descended. If this does not happen, neutering will be advised because the condition carries an increased chance of testicular tumors.

Testicular tumor

In older dogs, there may be a noticeable disparity in the size of the testicles. The development of a testicular tumor will often make one testicle large and firm while the other shrinks down and becomes flabby. Treatment is to remove both testicles, but will not cure a tumor that has spread.

Neutering

If you do not intend to breed your dog, he or she can be neutered before reaching sexual maturity. In females, neutering avoids such problems as womb infections and growths in the ovaries and womb. In male dogs, neutering prevents testicular growths, and is often advised for a young dog who starts to show inappropriate behavior such as mounting people's legs and running off after females in heat. The metabolism in dogs of either sex slows down after neutering, so aim for your pet to be at the correct body weight beforehand.

Urinary tract disorders

Problems in the urinary tract will rapidly affect your dog's general health and need fast diagnosis. Look out for any change in his normal intake of water and output of urine, because this could be an early warning sign.

Your **dog's health**

Signs of a problem

- ■ Squatting or cocking leg frequently but passing only a few spots of urine
- ■ Frequently passing a large volume of urine (polyuria)
- ■ Change in color of urine from normal pale yellow
- ■ Abdominal pain
- ■ Increased thirst (polydipsia), drinking more than 1.6oz of water per pound of body weight over a 24-hour period. (This is easy to measure if your dog is the only household pet and not drinking from an outside water source such as a pond.)

Cystitis

Bladder infections (cystitis) tend to be more common in females, because the female urethra, the tube that carries urine from the bladder, is shorter than in male dogs, making it easier for bacteria to enter the body. A dog with cystitis may repeatedly pass only a small amount of urine, which may contain blood and look pink. If you can collect a urine sample (see box, opposite) it will help diagnosis; otherwise, your vet may take a sample directly from the bladder. If infection is present, the vet will prescribe an appropriate antibiotic.

▷ **Excessive thirst**
If your dog spends a long time standing drinking over the water bowl, or repeatedly visiting it, then he may have an excessive thirst that could be linked to a bladder or kidney problem.

It is important to find any underlying cause for cystitis. For example, glucose in the urine associated with diabetes mellitus can increase susceptibility to bladder infections. A less common cause of bladder infection is a growth in the bladder wall. This may be detected by your vet palpating your dog's bladder, or during a bladder scan.

Urinary stones

Cystitis may also be associated with the presence of crystals in the urine, which can be seen under a microscope. A further complication is that urinary crystals can form into stones in the bladder. Your vet may be able to feel the stones manually and they can also be picked up by X-ray or an ultrasound scan. Some bladder stones can be dissolved with medication, but other types have to be removed surgically. Extracted stones are analyzed in a laboratory to determine how to prevent further stones from forming.

If a stone passes from the bladder, a male dog's urethra may become blocked because it is a long and narrow tube (unlike a female's urethra, which is short and wide). This situation requires urgent veterinary attention. Not only is the condition extremely painful, but it prevents the passage of urine out of

"It is important to **differentiate** between a **house-training lapse** and **incontinence.**"

△ **Bladder infections are uncomfortable**
Having cystitis is unpleasant and can make a
normally active dog feel under the weather and
disinterested in exercise.

the bladder, leading to pressure
backing up to the kidneys and
damaging them.

Prostatic disease

The prostate, the sex gland lying
around the urethra of the male
dog, is prone to various disorders.
Bacterial infection ascending from
the urethra can cause swelling and
inflammation of the prostate.
Symptoms may include blood
dripping from the penis, urinary
incontinence or difficulty passing
urine, abdominal pain, and
straining to pass feces. Infection
is treated with antibiotics and
castration. Swelling can also
be caused by benign prostatic

enlargement, which occurs in
an unneutered dog and is treated
by castration. Rarely, prostate
enlargement is due to a tumor,
especially in castrated dogs.

Urinary incontinence

It is important to differentiate
between a house-training lapse,
when your dog consciously empties
his bladder but just cannot get
outside in time, and incontinence,
where urine leaks out when your
dog is relaxed or asleep. In a puppy,
incontinence may be due to a
congenital anatomical problem, for
which surgical treatment may be
possible. Some dogs may become
incontinent after neutering, and
some require long-term medication;
incontinence in old age can also be
controlled medically to some extent.
Your vet will want to check that
there is no underlying disease.

Urine testing

A useful specimen to take to the
vet is a sample of the first urine
your dog passes in the morning.
Use a resealable container and be
prepared to move quickly to catch
the stream as your pet squats or
cocks a leg. Your vet can provide
a "collection kit" to make it easier.

Kidney disease

The kidneys—which filter waste
from the blood—are susceptible to
infection and can be affected by
some inherited diseases. Kidney
failure is common in old dogs.
Signs of disease include increased
thirst and urination with weight
loss, poor appetite, and vomiting
developing later. Urine and blood
tests help identify the cause.

Nervous system disorders

The nervous system comprises the brain and spinal cord, and the nerve pathways that carry signals throughout the body. Disorders can occur in any part of this system, affecting the way a dog moves and behaves.

Juvenile epilepsy

Convulsions, or seizures, are caused by electrical disturbances in the brain and can occur in a dog at any age (pp.158–9). However, if a dog first has seizures while he is young, then a disorder known as juvenile epilepsy is suspected. Blood is usually taken to rule out other causes for them such as liver disease. If the blood results are normal, juvenile epilepsy tends to be the diagnosis, especially in breeds known to be prone to the disorder, such as the Beagles, Border Collies, German Shepherds, Golden and Labrador Retrievers, and Irish Setters. Antiepileptic drugs will be needed for life.

Wobbler syndrome

Caused by a malformation of the neck bones putting pressure on the spinal cord, wobbler syndrome makes a dog move in an abnormal way, taking short steps with his front legs and wandering, wobbly steps with his back legs. He may also have neck pain. There are two forms of wobbler syndrome: one appears at an early age in giant breeds such as Great Danes and gradually worsens; the other form occurs in Dobermans and does not appear until middle age. The diagnosis is confirmed by X-rays and MRI. Treatment with corticosteroids may help and in some cases, surgery is advised.

Hydrocephalus

This is a congenital problem (present from birth) that occurs in Chihuahuas, Pekingese, and Boston Terriers among others. In hydrocephalus, the fluid that flows round the brain and spinal cord to protect them from injury, is prevented from draining away

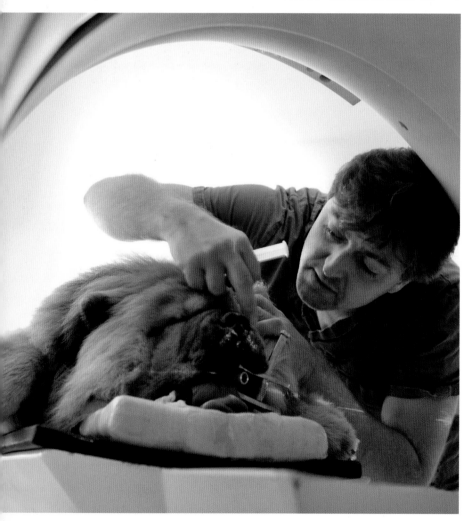

◁ **CT scanning**
Combining computer technology with X-rays, CT scanning detects abnormalities by producing images of the body in cross section, and is invaluable for investigating brain disorders.

▷ **Problems in the Chihuahua**
Syringomyelia, a brain disorder which affects a dog's gait and posture, is inherited in dome-headed breeds such as the Chihuahua.

▽ **Susceptible to seizures**
The German Shepherd is one of several breeds known to be at risk of juvenile epilepsy. Drug treatment is used to manage the disorder.

normally. The buildup of fluid leads to pressure inside the skull and the risk of brain damage. Severely affected puppies, which often do not survive long after birth, have a markedly domed skull, and fail to grow and develop like their littermates. Mild cases of hydrocephalus may not be recognized until a dog is older.

MRI or CT scanning, or possibly ultrasound imaging, will confirm the diagnosis. Drug treatment may reduce fluid production; it may also be possible to insert a shunt (tube) in the brain to drain excess fluid.

IVS

Often mistakenly called a stroke by owners, Ideopathic Vestibular Syndrome (IVS) usually occurs in old dogs, affecting the center of balance within the inner ear. The dog suddenly develops a head tilt and may lose his balance. His eyes flick from side to side as they try to stop the world from spinning. Some dogs are so badly affected that they are nauseous, vomit, and walk around in circles.

IVS usually resolves on its own after a few days. Your vet may give a drug to reduce nausea if your dog cannot keep down food and water. A drug that promotes blood supply to the brain is available and can help to prevent the disease.

CDRM

This distressing disease—chronic degenerative radiculomyelopathy (CDRM)—affects the spinal cord. It causes a dog to gradually lose coordination and movement of his hind limbs, even though he is otherwise well and retains voluntary control over his bladder and bowels. Breeds in which CDRM occurs include German Shepherds, Boxers, and Corgis. There is no treatment, other than helping the dog to cope.

Syringomyelia

SM, as this disease is known, is characterized by head and neck pain that may be hard to localize. A dog may sleep with his head in a strange position, have pain when being picked up, or have difficulty going up stairs. The classic sign is for the dog to walk along kicking with a hindleg as if to scratch his ear. The commonest cause of SM is a structural defect in the brain that results in a mismatch between brain size and the space in the skull. This is an inherited disorder in dome-headed breeds such as Spaniels, Chihuahuas, and Petit Basset Griffon Vendeens.

Definitive diagnosis requires an MRI scan, which is also used for screening. Treatment aims at pain control, with lifestyle changes such as feeding from a raised bowl and walking on the lead with a body harness rather than a collar. Surgery is also possible.

Hormonal disorders

Hormones are chemicals released into the bloodstream by various glands to carry messages to body tissues and organs. Most hormonal disorders occur through overproduction or underproduction of these chemicals.

Signs of a problem

■ Increased thirst (needing water bowl filled more often; drinking from ponds or puddles)

■ Change in appetite (increase or decrease)

■ Change in coat (altered color, different texture, hair loss)

■ Recurrent skin infections

■ Weight gain, weight loss, or inability to lose or gain weight (changes may be subtle, developing over a long time)

■ Lethargy and tiredness (may not be related to aging)

Diabetes mellitus

Insulin is a hormone produced by the pancreas to control the level of glucose in the blood. A deficiency in insulin results in diabetes mellitus, or "sugar diabetes."

Common signs of diabetes mellitus are ravenous hunger, weight loss, abnormal thirst, and frequent passing of large volumes of urine. Occasionally, the first indication may be loss of vision due to a cataract (clouding of the lens of the eye). Sometimes, the disorder may not be diagnosed until a dog becomes unwell from complications arising from diabetes mellitus and has to undergo examinations.

Diabetes mellitus is treated with injections of insulin, together with regular feeding and exercise. Many owners are initially worried about injecting their dogs, but this soon becomes part of the daily routine.

A female may develop diabetes mellitus after being in heat. Neutering may be the cure, provided there are enough insulin-producing cells remaining in the pancreas. Obesity is another risk factor for developing diabetes mellitus. The disorder seems to be more common in certain breeds, such as the miniature and toy poodles, some terriers, and Samoyeds.

△ **Tired all the time**
If your dog seems to be sleeping more than usual and is generally less active, he may not be slowing up with age but have a health problem such as an underactive thyroid.

▷ **Excessive thirst**
An increased thirst is a common sign of a hormonal disorder such as diabetes mellitus or Cushing's syndrome.

Hypothyroidism

In this condition, there is underproduction of the hormones produced by the thyroid gland in the neck. Hypothyroidism tends to develop in middle-aged dogs, but may appear at a younger age in breeds predisposed to the disorder, such as Irish Setters, English Sheepdogs, Dobermans, and Boxers. Hypothyroidism can have diverse effects. Typical signs of an underactive thyroid gland include weight gain that is difficult to reverse and lethargy. There may be changes in coat color, thinning of the coat leading to fur loss, and skin infections. Hypothyroidism is diagnosed from blood tests and treated with thyroid hormone replacement, given by tablet.

Cushing's syndrome

Mostly seen in middle-aged or older dogs, Cushing's syndrome is the result of abnormally high blood levels of cortisol—a hormone produced by the adrenal glands. Signs are increased appetite and thirst, increased urination, hair loss, development of a pot-belly, and blackheads on the skin. There may be slow healing of wounds, breathlessness, and lethargy. Diagnosis is based on blood and urine tests, X-rays, and ultrasound. Treatment is usually with drugs; if an adrenal tumor is the cause of the high cortisol levels, surgery may be possible.

Addison's disease

In Addison's disease the adrenal glands do not produce enough of the hormones cortisol and aldosterone. The deficiency interferes with the balance of sodium and potassium in the blood, and affects the ability to cope with stress. The disease typically affects

Living with Addison's disease
A dog with Addison's disease can lead a normal life once he receives treatment. In stressful situations, such as going to a kennel, he may require additional drugs to help him cope.

young or middle-aged female dogs and is sometimes caused by sudden withdrawal of corticosteroid drugs.

Signs of Addison's disease can be vague: vomiting, diarrhea, loss of appetite, weight loss, and increased thirst. Occasionally, these signs become much more severe, and the dog collapses in a so-called "Addisonian crisis." Diagnosis is by blood and urine tests; treatment involves hormone replacement with tablets, and monitoring with regular blood screening.

Dwarfism

The hormone that regulates growth is produced by the pituitary gland, situated just beneath the brain.

In the congenital disorder known as dwarfism, there is underproduction of this growth hormone and normal development is affected. In a puppy with dwarfism, the head, body, and limbs may all be in proportion but undersized; or just one area of the body, such as the legs, may be abnormal. The adult coat does not grow, so alopecia develops as the puppy coat is lost and not replaced. The dog has a shrill bark, and may show no signs of sexual maturity.

Dwarfism can be treated with injections of growth hormone together with supplementation of thyroid hormone. Affected dogs have a shortened lifespan.

Immune system disorders

The normal role of the immune system is to fight disease and protect the body from harm. When it goes wrong, the system may not provide enough protection, or it may become overactive and cause a disorder itself.

Signs of a problem

- Itchy skin (allergy)
- Swelling of lymph nodes (lymphoma)
- Lethargy
- High temperature
- Scales and crusting on nose (discoid lupus erythematosus)
- Spontaneous bleeding (thrombocytopenia)

Allergies

An allergy is an overreaction of the immune system to a substance usually considered harmless (an allergen). Flea allergic dermatitis is a common skin disorder in dogs (p.110) resulting from an allergic response to flea saliva. Some dogs react to environmental allergens, such as pollen, that are inhaled or come into contact with the skin. Hypersensitivity to certain foods can also cause a reaction.

Typically, signs of an allergy—most commonly, itchy skin—first appear in the young dog. Strict flea control is vital, and a food trial to identify any food hypersensitivity may make it easier to avoid trigger foods. Treatment is based on shampoos, antibiotics for skin infections, and drugs such as antihistamines or low-dose corticosteroids to reduce the allergic response. Allergens can be identified with skin testing and specific blood tests so that a vaccine can be formulated.

Lymphoma

The lymph nodes are the sentinels of the immune system. These small organs work as filters, trapping bacteria and other harmful substances before they enter the bloodstream. Enlargement of the lymph nodes may be due to injury or infection; more seriously, it can mean a type of cancer known as lymphoma. In dogs, lymphoma may be seen or felt as swellings under either side of the jaw or in front of a shoulder. If the disease has reached an advanced stage, the dog may also be drinking excessively. Diagnosis requires biopsy of an enlarged lymph node, blood tests, X-rays, and ultrasound scanning. Chemotherapy can be successful in treating lymphoma, especially with an early diagnosis.

◁ **Allergy prone**
The Japanese Akita is a breed particularly prone to skin allergies. Signs of a possible allergic reaction include excessive licking and scratching all over.

△ **Springer Spaniel puppy at risk**
Immune-mediated hemolytic anemia occurs in many breeds, including the English Springer Spaniel. The disease may develop gradually or arise suddenly, with pale gums and lethargy.

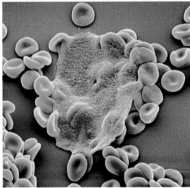

△ **Destruction of red blood cells**
A large blood cell (macrophage) in the immune system destroys the body's own red blood cells, causing immune-mediated hemolytic anemia.

Immune-mediated disorders

Rarely, the immune system may direct itself against the body's own tissues. This causes a variety of serious diseases, among which is systemic lupus erythematosus (SLE), an inflammatory condition that causes blood-clotting problems, joint pain, skin changes, and seizures. Diagnosis may involve blood tests, skin biopsy, and examination of joint fluid. SLE is treated with immunosuppressive drugs. Another form of lupus, cutaneous or discoid lupus erythematosus (DLE) affects the dog's nose, and sometimes other areas of skin, causing scaling, crusting, depigmentation, and ulceration. DLE is diagnosed from skin biopsies. Treatment with creams or ointments may help in mild cases, but immunosuppressive drugs are needed for severe DLE.

Immune-mediated hemolytic anemia is caused by the destruction of red blood cells. This disease can be due to another immune disorder such as SLE, infection, or drug treatment. Breeds that are particularly prone include Springer Spaniels and Cocker Spaniels. Signs include lethargy, weakness, pale gums, and fever. Diagnosis is from blood tests, X-rays, and ultrasound scanning. This disorder is treated with corticosteroids, specific treatment of an underlying cause if possible, and blood transfusion.

In immune-mediated thrombocytopenia, there is a low blood platelet count (platelets are the smallest blood cells), which affects normal blood clotting. Signs include pinpoint hemorrhages under the skin, nosebleeds, and bleeding gums. Breeds predisposed to this disorder include Cocker Spaniels and Poodles. Diagnosis is by blood test, and treatment consists of immunosuppressive drug therapy.

External parasites

Even the most well-groomed dog is susceptible to infestation by various skin parasites, some of which are potential carriers of serious diseases. Year-round prevention is the key to controlling these pests.

Signs of a problem

- Scratching
- Bare patches where hair falls out
- Scabs and crusting
- Seeing the actual parasite
- Black debris (flea dirt, which leave telltale red streaks when dissolved in water)
- Effects of disease caused by parasite (e.g., in Lyme disease carried by ticks: painful, swollen joints, fever, failure to eat, lethargy, swollen lymph glands; more rarely, neck pain, seizures, kidney failure, heart problems)

Fleas

You need to take year-round preventive action against fleas. Running a flea comb through your dog's coat, especially over the rump, may catch fleas, which you can kill by squashing them against the teeth of the comb with a finger. You are more likely to find flea dirt, which show up as black debris. Treatment can be topical (applied to the skin at the back of the neck), tablets, and collars. Alternatively, you can spray, wash, or powder your dog. Treat all other pets, including cats and rabbits, at the same time as your dog. Fleas spend

most of their life cycle in carpets and furniture, so you may need to use separate products to eradicate them from the home.

Ticks

These unpleasant creatures are a seasonal problem that mostly occurs in spring and fall. Ticks can attach themselves to your dog and may transmit diseases; for example, some ticks carry the bacterium *Borrelia burgdorferi,* acquired from mammals such as rodents and deer, which causes Lyme disease in humans and dogs.

Swift removal of a tick reduces the risk of infections. Using tweezers, hold the tick close to the dog's skin but without squeezing its body. Gently twist to remove it. If the head is embedded, try to remove that too. Mouthparts left behind can cause a reaction and a lump may develop, but treatment is not usually needed and the lump will vanish.

If you live in or are traveling to an area known for ticks, you should take preventive measures such as topical treatments and collars.

Mites

The spiderlike *Sarcoptes* mite is commonly passed on to dogs from foxes. It particularly affects the

ears, elbows, and hocks, causing sarcoptic mange with intense itchiness, hair loss, and skin sores.

Demodex mites are probably passed from mother to puppies at birth. They affect the skin on the head and around the eyes, and can appear elsewhere, causing fur thinning, bald areas, and a musty smell. These mites may be found in skin scrapings from healthy dogs, but they particularly occur at times of stress or illness when a dog's immune system is weakened. Mild demodectic mange resolves without treatment. Severe cases need specific treatment to kill the mites, which is continued until several skin scrapings are clear; antibiotics may also be needed if there is an associated skin infection.

The bright orange, non-parasitic harvest mite is picked up by a dog running in fields in the summer. It tends to be found on the skin of the toes, ears, and around the eyes. Harvest mites rub off easily and usually cause no reaction, but they may be linked to a serious disorder called seasonal canine illness.

Lice

A dog who has lice will scratch frequently. The lice can be seen in the coat and on the skin, with nits (eggs) attached to hairs. The entire life cycle of a louse takes place on an individual dog and lasts less than three weeks. Lice are transferred by close contact to other dogs or via grooming tools, but not to people. Your vet will recommend specific treatments.

▷ **Skin parasites**
Lice, fleas, and ticks are common parasites. All are nuisances, and ticks can transmit disease. Preventive measures and regular checks of your dog's coat keep these pests to a minimum.

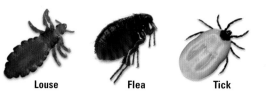

Louse　　**Flea**　　**Tick**

Flea hunt
If your dog persistently bites or scratches his coat he is highly likely to be bothered by fleas. These pests cause maddening irritation as they move around and feed on their host's blood.

Internal parasites

Worms that live inside your pet are common and they can be controlled easily with regular treatment. Prevention of internal parasites, rather than having to treat an infestation and its effects, is preferable.

Roundworm

The adult worms, which look like strands of spaghetti, live in the gut, producing eggs that pass out in the feces and mature for one to three weeks before being infectious to others, including humans. This is why picking up your dog's feces is so important. A dog can acquire roundworms from the soil or by eating other carriers such as rodents. Puppies can be infected in the womb by roundworm larvae passed on by their mother.

Prevention of roundworms starts with treating the pregnant dog and continues after birth, both with the puppies and their mother, and at regular intervals throughout life. Ask your vet about which product to use and the worming schedule to follow as your puppy grows up.

Tapeworm

The eggs of the most common tapeworm species, *Dipylidium caninum*, are carried by fleas and your dog can become infected by licking fleas off his coat and

▽ **Healthy family**
Roundworm prevention for these puppies started before they were born, since their mother was treated during pregnancy. They should be wormed regularly throughout life.

△ **Danger in snails**
Lungworm can be picked up if a dog eats an infected snail or slug, either intentionally or accidentally if, for example, there is one on a toy or bowl left outside.

△ **Sources of tapeworms**
Dogs are most likely to pick up tapeworms from infected fleas, but other sources of infestation include contaminated raw meat and the carcasses of wildlife such as rodents.

swallowing them. The adult flat, segmented worm develops within the gut, and sheds egg-containing segments, which you may see as wriggly "rice grains" around your dog's anus or in his feces. They cause itching, and your dog may "scoot" his bottom along the ground. Treatment is a tapeworm-specific medication, together with flea control.

Your dog may pick up other tapeworm species from eating raw meat or animal parts, wild animals, or roadkill. Some tapeworms are a serious health risk to humans.

Lungworm
Also known as French heartworm, this parasite (*Angiostrongylus vasorum*) is picked up by a dog eating snails and slugs, which can carry the worm larvae. Adult worms develop in the right ventricle (chamber) of the heart and in the pulmonary artery. The females lay eggs containing first-stage larvae, which are carried in the bloodstream to the lungs. Here, they hatch out, burrowing into lung tissue and causing

damage. The dog coughs them up and swallows them, passing them out in feces as a source of further infection to slugs and snails.

Lungworm can be hard to diagnose. Various symptoms may include lethargy, cough, anemia, nose bleeds, weight loss, poor appetite, vomiting, and diarrhea. The dog may also display behavioral changes. Diagnostic tests include examining a tracheal wash and feces, as well as X-rays and blood tests.

Your vet will recommend drugs for treatment and prevention of lungworm. Pick up dog feces promptly (and fox droppings, too, if you find them in the garden). Lungworm cannot be passed directly to other pets or to humans.

Heartworm
This parasite (*Dirofilaria immitis*) is transmitted by the bite of an infected mosquito. Heartworms

live in the dog's heart, lungs, and surrounding blood vessels, and can cause death if left untreated. Owners in high-risk areas should seek prompt veterinary attention if their dog develops a cough or becomes lethargic during the mosquito season. Diagnosis is by blood test and treatment is risky, requiring the dog to rest for several weeks afterward. Year-round prevention with heartworm medicines is usually effective.

Preventing worms
Routine worming reduces the likelihood of infestation. Your vet will advise you on the best treatment for your puppy or dog. The ideal program depends on the perceived risk, which may be high if, for example, you walk your dog in public places, he is an avid scavenger of dead rodents, or he lives with small children. Strict flea control is the key to tapeworm prevention. You must weigh your dog, especially if he is still growing, so that you give the correct dose.

Infectious diseases

Most infectious diseases are caused by bacteria and viruses. Just as in humans, bacterial infections in dogs are treated with antibiotics, while many serious viral infections can be avoided with vaccinations.

Your dog's health

Signs of a problem

■ Diarrhea (sometimes bloody), vomiting, and abdominal pains

■ Runny nose, coughing, discharge from eyes (distemper)

■ Hardening of paw pads and nose (distemper)

■ Loss of appetite

■ Weakness, collapse

■ Fever

■ Hemorrhages under the skin, nosebleeds (leptospirosis)

▽ **Vulnerable age groups**
A dog's age can make a difference to his ability to resist illness or cope with the effects. Very young puppies and very old dogs are most at risk from infectious diseases.

Parvovirus

This dangerous viral infection is typically seen in young dogs that often have not been vaccinated or have not yet completed their series of vaccinations. Parvovirus causes acute gastroenteritis, with bloody diarrhea and vomiting, and can be fatal within just two to three days. The virus, which can survive for months in the environment, is transmitted via infected feces.

Parvovirus is diagnosed by testing for the virus in feces as well as by the history and signs of illness. Treatment relies on intensive intravenous fluid therapy, together with a drug to prevent vomiting and antibiotics to prevent secondary bacterial infection.

Distemper

A highly infectious viral disease, distemper is transmitted through airborne droplets and spreads readily between dogs, especially if they are young and unvaccinated. Initially, the disorder affects the respiratory tract, causing a runny nose, coughing, and discharge from the eyes. Later there is vomiting and diarrhea, and hardening of the dog's paw pads and nose. The virus is not long-lived in the environment and is easily killed by most household disinfectants.

Diagnosis is from the history and signs. Treatment consists of antibiotics for secondary infection, and intravenous fluids and antiemetics for gastroenteritis.

◁ **Passing on infections**
Dogs are sociable and their habit of sniffing each other, and other dogs' urine and droppings, means that infections can spread rapidly among unvaccinated animals.

▽ **Danger on the streets**
Feral dogs roam the streets in many parts of the world, some of them infected with rabies. They should never be handled, however appealing they may seem.

Leptospirosis

Passed on through the urine of an infected animal, leptospirosis is a highly infectious bacterial disease that both dogs and humans can contract. One form, *Leptospira icterohaemorrhagiae* causes Weil's disease, mainly targeting the liver; it is carried by rats, so dogs can pick up the infection directly from the urine of an infected rat, or when swimming in ditches and ponds. *L. canicola* is a dog-specific variant that affects the kidneys. Signs can include vomiting, bloody diarrhea, weakness, and fever.

Leptospirosis is diagnosed from blood and urine tests. Treatment requires long-term antibiotics and intravenous fluids, and the dog must be nursed in isolation.

Rabies

The rabies virus, which can also infect humans, is transmitted in saliva through the bite of an infected animal, although being bitten does not inevitably lead to development of the disease. Rabies can cause seizures, painful throat spasms, and paralysis, and once the disease has developed, it is nearly always fatal. Diagnosis is based on the history and signs of illness (and can be confirmed by a postmortem examination of the brain). Fortunately, the vaccines now available for both humans and dogs are very effective.

Campylobacter and salmonella

These are both bacterial diseases characterized by gastroenteritis, and can be passed either way between humans and dogs. The initial infection is acquired from contaminated food or water.

Diagnosis of campylobacter and salmonella is from testing fresh fecal samples. These diseases are treated with intravenous fluid therapy, and specific antibiotics. Preventive measures against infection include avoiding raw and undercooked meat and covering all food against flies.

Vaccination

Protecting your dog against infection is one of the best things you can do for him. Vaccinations have greatly reduced the incidence of major canine diseases such as parvovirus and distemper and prevent other infections, including rabies and leptospirosis. During pregnancy, a female with up-to-date vaccinations passes immunity on to her pups. This protection lasts for a few weeks after birth, then the puppies should be vaccinated. Your vet will recommend when boosters should be given. Some vaccines can give up to three years protection against certain diseases, following a booster 12 months after the initial dose.

"Viral diseases spread readily between dogs, especially the young and unvaccinated."

Alternative therapies

Many veterinarians use alternative therapies, often also referred to as complementary therapies, alongside conventional medicine. Ask your vet if such treatments could be of benefit to your dog.

Manipulative therapy

A few types of complementary therapy can be applied to animals by practitioners who are not registered veterinarians. These are forms of manipulation such as osteopathy, chiropractic, and physical therapy, which may help a back problem, for example. Your dog must, however, be referred to a practitioner by a vet who has examined him, reached a diagnosis, and decided that he may benefit from manipulative treatment of this kind.

Acupuncture

Only a registered veterinarian who has undergone specific training may perform acupuncture on an animal. In this therapy, thin, solid needles are inserted into specific areas of the body referred to as acupuncture points, blocking pain signals, and trigger points. Acupuncture is also believed to stimulate the release of endorphins, body chemicals that act as natural painkillers and also increase feelings of well-being.

Acupuncture is particularly useful for dogs with chronic pain associated with arthritis or injuries, for example; it may also help with other problems, although this role is less recognized. The therapy is usually tolerated very well by dogs, especially if they are coaxed with food while treatment is taking place. The needles will be left in place for up to 30 minutes, and may be moved to provide additional stimulation. The dog can move around with the needles in place, or lie down. Some dogs

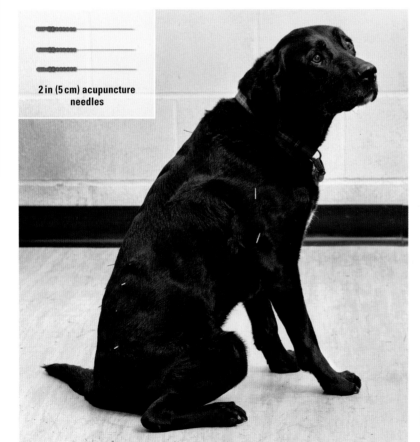

2 in (5 cm) acupuncture needles

◁ **Acupuncture**
The needles used in acupuncture are sterile and disposable, a fresh set being used for each dog. How many are used, where they are inserted, how long they are left in place, and how much they are moved, determine the treatment "dose."

▽ **Physical therapy**
Your vet may refer your dog for physical therapy to help him recover after surgery or an injury. Elderly dogs with arthritic joints can also benefit from this treatment.

become very sleepy during the acupuncture session and may sleep for a while afterward.

For a day or so after having acupuncture, it is not unusual for symptoms to become worse, rather than improving. If the deterioration persists, your dog's therapist will adjust the treatment at the next session. There are some dogs who do not respond to acupuncture at all, just as there are humans for whom the therapy has no benefit.

Acupuncture sessions are usually weekly at first, with your dog's progress and response being monitored. According to what suits the individual dog, treatments will probably then be spaced further apart.

Hydrotherapy

Swimming is a non-weight-bearing form of exercise that is very beneficial for joint problems and can also help with weight-loss, stamina, and building up muscle

after surgery, for example. Hydrotherapy adds to these benefits by providing controlled conditions for water-based exercises. Most dogs enjoy using the facilities at a hydrotherapy center, which can vary from a simple pool to an aquatic treadmill. The pool water will be heated to a comfortably warm temperature, and its quality is monitored

regularly. There will be facilities for drying your dog off afterward to prevent him from becoming cold and stiffening up.

Your vet will refer your dog for hydrotherapy if it looks likely that treatment will be of benefit. Ideally, anyone offering hydrotherapy for dogs should be qualified and registered with an appropriate professional organization.

▷ **Hydrotherapy**
If your dog likes swimming, you should have no difficulty with him accepting hydrotherapy, which offers carefully planned, supervised exercises in warm water.

Herbal and homeopathic treatments

Only a registered veterinarian may treat a dog with herbal and homeopathic therapies. Herbal medicine, which is based on natural substances, may sound innocuous but remedies can include very powerful active agents that can be dangerous in certain circumstances, for example when taken in conjunction with other drugs. Many common health problems in dogs, ranging from allergies to arthritis, skin disorders, and anxiety, may respond to herbal remedies. If you use herbal medicines for your dog, follow your vet's instructions carefully. Homeopathy treats the underlying disease process, not the outward signs, and takes a holistic approach that includes character and lifestyle. This therapy is based on the theory of using "like to cure like," where a substance that causes certain symptoms in a healthy body can, when given in minute doses, cure illnesses that cause the same signs.

△ **Homeopathic remedies**
Many homeopathic medicines are available in liquid form and can be dropped directly onto the dog's tongue or added to water.

Nursing a sick dog

There may come a time when your dog needs nursing because he is ill or recovering from surgery and cannot manage things he usually does on his own. Follow your vet's instructions and ask for advice if in doubt.

Home care after surgery

Dogs are rarely kept in overnight after neutering or other routine operations, but the vet will give you advice on any specific health care that is needed. Your dog may be discharged with medication such as pain relief, but if he seems uncomfortable then contact the vet. Exercise immediately after surgery should be restricted unless you are advised otherwise.

Contrary to popular belief, a dog does more harm than good if he licks at an undressed wound, which can become sore and infected. Most dogs accept wearing an Elizabethan collar or similar device, and anti-lick strips can also deter an inquisitive tongue and stop dogs from removing dressings on paws and legs.

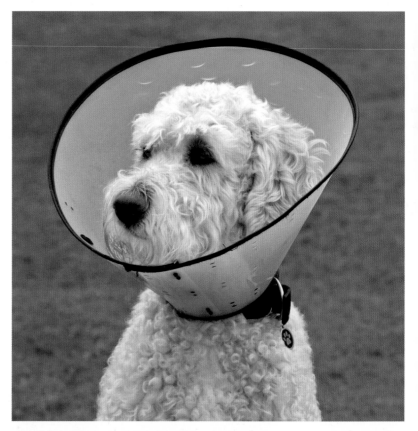

▷ **Elizabethan collar**
Your dog may not be able to reach his food and water bowls while wearing an Elizabethan collar so you may need to remove it periodically.

△ ▷ **Adding medicine to food**
This is an easy way to give your dog medication, provided he eats the food. Check the directions first: some medications need to be taken on an empty stomach or must not be crushed.

Keep dressings clean and dry by covering with a boot or plastic bag when you take your dog outside to do his business. If he worries at a dressing excessively, or it becomes smelly or soiled, then seek your vet's advice as soon as possible.

Giving medication

Prescribed medication should be given to your dog as directed by your vet, and only by an adult. Make sure other pets do not take a drug accidentally, especially if it is given in food. If your dog is prescribed an antibiotic, it is important that he completes the full course. A liquid medication may need to be shaken to ensure thorough mixing before the dose is given. If you are injecting your dog with, for example, insulin, then strictly follow your vet's instructions about storage and administration.

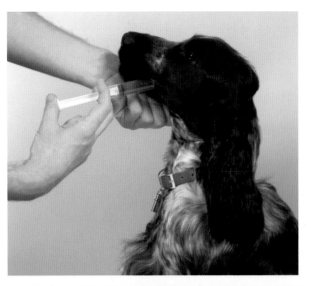

◁ **Liquid medicine**
If the prescribed medication is a suspension, shake the bottle to ensure thorough mixing. Remove the dose and give to your dog directly into his mouth or with food.

▽ **Sleeping it off**
Following surgery your dog will probably spend more time asleep than usual. Find him a cozy place, where he can let his body recover.

> "A **post-operative** dog needs **rest** in a **warm**, quiet, undisturbed **place**."

Giving medication directly by mouth is ideal, since you will be sure that your dog has swallowed it. Speak to your vet if this is difficult; some medications can be hidden in food or a treat (although not if they must be taken on an empty stomach). Unless the tablet is palatable, avoid crushing and mixing it with food, since your dog may then refuse to eat and will not receive the medication. Some tablets must only be given whole.

If your dog develops symptoms such as an upset stomach (vomiting or diarrhea) while on medication, then discontinue the treatment until you have spoken to a vet.

Food and water

Ensure your dog can reach his food and water bowls comfortably, perhaps raising them off the ground so that he has no need to reach down. You may be given a prescription diet to help your dog's recovery but if he will not eat it ask your vet about alternative suitable foods. A similar problem may occur with your dog refusing to drink recommended rehydration fluids. In this case, encourage him to drink cooled, boiled water, which is better than taking no fluids at all.

Rest and exercise

A post-operative dog needs to rest in a quiet place at a warm, not hot, temperature with comfortable bedding. He may prefer to sleep away from the family, or he may seek company. Short walks just puttering around the yard are also important to keep the joints, bladder, and bowel functioning.

Caring for an **elderly dog**

It is hard to accept that a beloved dog is showing the effects of aging, but you can help him to go on enjoying life, albeit at a slower pace. A little extra care can make a big difference to your senior dog's well-being.

Feeling comfortable

Older dogs tend to be more affected than younger ones by extremes of temperature. Small dogs and naturally lean, thin-coated breeds like greyhounds and whippets may feel the cold more as they age and will benefit from wearing a coat in chilly weather. Remember to remove the coat when your dog is in warmer surroundings or else he will overheat, and never leave a dog in a wet coat. If the weather is particularly warm, a desk fan is a comfort to an overheated dog.

Diet and exercise

Your senior dog will naturally sleep more and be less active, but it is important not to let him become overweight. Combat a spreading

△ **Raised food bowl**
Simply raising your dog's feeding bowl may restore his enjoyment of eating. You can buy a stand or improvise with blocks or a step.

▽ **Wrapping up**
Keep your senior dog warm in a coat chosen from the wide range available, or make one yourself from a blanket.

waistline with regular exercise and senior foods specially formulated to be less energy-dense. Frequent short walks are more suitable than one daily marathon if your dog is struggling to keep up. Very elderly dogs can just putter in the yard and rest whenever they want.

Your dog's mobility may start to be restricted by arthritis. He may find it difficult to jump into the car or to negotiate steps. Lift him into the car if he is not too heavy, or teach him to use a ramp instead. Ramps can also be placed over steps to convert them into a gentle incline. If your dog's neck is stiff, raising his food and water bowls on special stands (or improvising with bricks) should help him to eat and drink comfortably. If an arthritic

▷ **Taking it easy**
Take your older dog for frequent short walks over a familiar route, on a lead if he needs the security. Be prepared to amble at his pace.

dog finds it hard to curl around to fit in his basket, spread a bigger area of firm and supportive bedding directly on the floor.

An elderly dog needs grooming more often when he cannot reach around to clean himself effectively. Keep the grooming sessions short to avoid tiring him.

Being stiff is painful. Ask your vet about joint supplements and medications that might help your dog to move more easily.

Senior clinic

Your veterinary practice may offer a senior clinic where the focus is on easing your dog through his later years. You will be given advice on such issues as ideal body weight, nutritional supplements, changes in behavior and eating habits, and

exercise. A clinic can help you to detect problems early and enable treatment to be started as soon as possible. For example, a simple test to assess how much your dog is drinking may provide the impetus for further investigation.

Senility and confusion

Many older dogs are in good physical health but showing signs of senility and confusion. Maintaining a daily routine in familiar surroundings helps them to feel secure. Your vet can tell you about drugs that may help.

◁ **Weight watching**
Monitoring your older dog's weight is a simple aid to good health. Unintentional weight loss may be an early sign of a problem.

Euthanasia

There may come a time when, after careful thought and consideration, you decide to have an old dog euthanized if his quality of life is poor. This can be performed only by a veterinary surgeon in the veterinary practice. A drug is given by intravenous injection into a front leg vein, and the vet may give your dog a sedative first. There may be involuntary movements and the bladder or bowels may empty, but many dogs pass away peacefully. It is a good idea to decide in advance how you want your dog's body handled afterward, rather than facing the issue on what will be a distressing day.

5

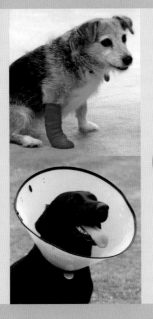

Canine
emergencies

Basic first aid

Dogs are inquisitive by nature and do not understand danger the way we do. It is impossible to prevent accidents from happening, so be prepared to provide emergency care if your dog, or someone else's, is injured.

Helping an injured dog

An injured dog usually needs to be examined by a veterinarian. If you know the basic rules of first aid, you will be able to provide help until the vet arrives, or the dog can be transported to a clinic.

When attending to an injured dog, you may need to muzzle him; if he is in pain and frightened, he may snap. Move him only if absolutely necessary or if you are sure moving him will not cause further injuries. In the case of bleeding, attempt to stem the flow of blood from any major wounds with direct pressure, carefully raising the injured area above the level of the heart if possible (pp.154–5).

Remember that there are parts of the world where dogs may have rabies. If you are in such an area and see a dog requiring help, you should keep at a safe distance and call an animal control organization.

At home, it is useful to keep your vet's telephone number somewhere handy: near the telephone, stored on your cell phone, or under a magnet on the refrigerator. Make sure you know what arrangements are in place for obtaining veterinary help if it is needed outside normal office hours.

Recovery position

If an injured dog is unconscious, put him in the recovery position. To do this, remove the dog's collar and place him on his right side, with his head and neck in line with his body. Gently pull his tongue forward to hang out of the side of his mouth. Feel for a heartbeat and a pulse on the inside of the thigh. Look for chest movement and feel for breath from the nostrils. If the dog is not breathing or his heart has stopped, start resuscitation.

Resuscitation

Hopefully, if you find yourself in a situation where a dog needs to be resuscitated, there will be someone to help you. It is important to stay calm, although this can be difficult.

A dog's heart may stop beating or his respiration fail following an accident involving electrocution or drowning, for example, or after a seizure. His best chance of recovery is at a veterinary practice but resuscitation needs to be started immediately once the need has been identified. Call a vet for advice or, ideally, ask someone else

First aid kit

Accidents can happen at any time, so always keep a few basic first aid necessities on hand. Compact kits equipped with a range of items for dealing with minor emergencies are readily available. These are particularly useful for taking in the car or carrying in a backpack on long walks.

First aid kit

Saline wash

Cotton balls

Thermometer

Disposable gloves

Adhesive bandage

Bandage

Scissors

△ In safe hands
The best place for an injured dog is obviously a veterinary office. But if you cannot take him there right away, you may be able to help him by using simple first aid.

to make the call while you place the dog in the recovery position. Before attempting resuscitation, check the airway for any obstruction at the back of the mouth.

If the dog is not breathing, start artificial respiration. Place your hands one over the other on the chest wall, just behind the shoulders. Apply a sharp downward movement every 3–5 seconds, allowing the chest wall to spring back in between each thrust, until voluntary breath movements occur.

Check for the dog's circulation by feeling for a pulse (on the inside of the thigh) and a heartbeat (on the side of the chest just behind the elbow). If the heart has stopped, begin cardiac massage.

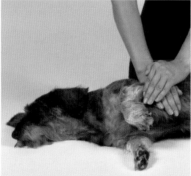

△ Resuscitation
If a dog's heart has stopped beating, his chances of recovery depend on resuscitation being started within a few minutes. Cardiac massage to keep the circulation going is a simple technique that can be lifesaving.

The massage technique varies according to the size of the dog.
■ Small dog—place the fingers and thumb of one hand around the dog's chest just behind the elbow and squeeze them together twice per second while your other hand is supporting the back.

■ Medium-sized dog—place the heel of one hand on the dog's chest just behind the elbow; place your other hand on top and press down on the chest approximately 80-100 times per minute.
■ Large or overweight dog—instead of placing him in the recovery position, lay the dog on his back with his head slightly lower than his body if possible. Place one hand on his chest over the lower end of the breastbone with your other hand on top and apply compressions directed toward the dog's head approximately 80-100 times per minute.

In all cases, check for a pulse after 15 seconds of applying compressions. If the heartbeat is still absent, continue with cardiac massage until you feel a pulse. If someone else is with you, they can give artificial respiration at the same time.

Deciding how long to continue resuscitation is difficult. If you can act quickly enough, you may keep the dog's brain adequately supplied with oxygen. But unless resuscitation starts within 3–4 minutes of the heart stopping, there is an increased likelihood of irreversible brain damage. In an ideal situation, a vet would pass a tube into the main airway to continue artificial respiration, and would give the dog drugs to help restore heart function.

Basic first aid

Wounds and burns

Never leave a wound to heal itself—even the smallest injury can become infected, especially when a dog licks it. If your dog has a severe wound or burns from any source, seek veterinary help as soon as possible.

Minor wounds

If a wound has been caused by another dog or pet then it should be seen by a vet as soon as possible, since it is likely to become infected. However, a small clean wound can be treated at home. Gently flush the wound with saline solution (commercial, or a teaspoon of salt dissolved in a half quart of warm water) to remove any dirt or debris. Carefully cut away hair from around the wound using blunt-ended scissors.

Apply a dressing or bandage, if possible, to prevent your dog from licking at the wound: you may think licking will help the wound to heal, but it is more likely to cause infection. Use appropriate materials if you have them on hand, or improvise with socks or tights to cover a wound on a limb, or a T-shirt for wounds on the chest or abdomen. Use adhesive tape rather than safety pins to hold a bandage in place. Take care not to apply the bandage too tightly, keep it dry, and change it regularly to check on the wound.

Always seek advice if you notice an offensive smell or if a discharge seeps through the bandage.

More serious wounds

A deep or extensive wound needs urgent veterinary attention. Call the vet practice to inform them of

◁ **Worrying at a wound**
A bandage protects a wound, especially from a dog's tongue, but if your dog will not leave it alone, he should wear an Elizabethan collar to prevent him from causing further damage.

the situation and to tell them when you are likely to arrive. Apply a temporary bandage as best you can to staunch the bleeding.

If the wound is on a limb, raise it above the level of the heart if possible, apply direct pressure via swabs or other padding, and bandage the pad in place. A tourniquet is not advised. Take great care if a foreign body is stuck in the wound: avoid pushing it in more deeply and do not attempt to remove it yourself.

For a wound on the chest, apply swabs soaked with warm saline solution or cooled boiled water and hold them in place with a bandage or a T-shirt.

A wound on the ear flap will spray blood whenever your dog shakes his head. Cover the wound with a swab and bandage the ear flap to his head (p.114).

Aftercare will depend on the nature of the wound. Bandages will need to be changed every 2–5 days as advised by your vet. All bandages must be kept dry, so cover them with a waterproof outer layer when your dog goes outside to relieve himself.

Burns

Painful and sometimes severe damage to the skin can be caused by contact with heat, electricity, or chemicals.

Burns from fire or a hot object such as an iron, or scalding with hot liquid are treated in the same way. Remove your dog from the source of the injury without endangering yourself, then contact your vet for advice; a burn or scald can be very serious, with hidden damage to deep tissues. Flood the area with cold water for at least ten minutes then cover with a moist sterile dressing or plastic wrap to prevent contamination and stop your dog from interfering with the burn. Keep him warm and as still as possible while taking him to the vet. He will be given pain relief, and treatment for shock if the area affected is extensive.

Electrical burns in the mouth through biting a power cable are common. Turn off the power at source before handling your dog. Urgent veterinary attention will be needed for pain relief and also because an electrical shock can cause dangerous complications.

If your dog has been burned by chemicals, take care not to contaminate yourself. Identify and write down the substances involved and contact your vet. If appropriate, the vet may advise you to flush the area with water, but you must be careful to avoid spreading the chemicals further.

> **"A wound** caused by **another dog or pet** should be **seen by a vet**—it is likely to **become infected."**

How to bandage a paw

Apply a sterile dressing. Run a soft conforming bandage down the front of the leg, over the paw, up behind, then back to the paw and up the front again.

Wind the bandage around the leg down to the paw and then back up the leg. Repeat the earlier steps with an elasticized gauze bandage.

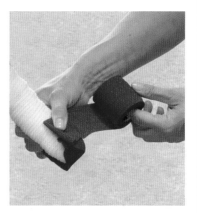

Repeat with a final cohesive layer, running it up on to the fur to secure it. Zinc oxide tape can also be used to secure the top of the dressing.

Dressing a wound
Minor wounds or cuts can be treated at home using sterile dressings and bandages, rather than needing a trip to the vet. Secure the bandage firmly but check that your puppy is comfortable with it on.

Seizures

Convulsions, or seizures, are due to abnormal electrical activity in the brain. In a young dog, the cause is likely to be epilepsy; reasons for seizures in an older dog vary but could include a brain tumor.

Signs of seizures

Seeing a dog have a convulsion or seizure is very alarming. All you can do is clear the area around your dog so that he cannot harm himself, and contact the vet for advice. Make a note of when the seizure occurred and any details that could be relevant, such as whether the television was on at the time, and whether your dog had eaten recently or just come back from a walk. If you have an unneutered female, note if it is around the time of her cycle.

Seizures classically occur when a dog is dozing. You may have noticed your dog acting strangely beforehand, but a seizure can also be totally unexpected. Signs of seizures may be trembling and twitching, or your dog may lie on his side, with his legs paddling as if he was running. (Dogs commonly do this when they are "dreaming," but they will respond when called or touched.) Your dog may also salivate and chomp his jaws, empty his bowels, and urinate. A seizure lasts from only seconds to a few minutes. Your dog may be aggressive during a seizure or in recovery. He may rapidly return to normal, but he could be distant and disoriented for a few hours.

A dog may have more than one seizure within a few hours or days of each other. More troubling, he may have a run of seizures, where he is not fully conscious between each episode. This is called status epilepticus and is a real emergency needing veterinary attention.

Treating seizures

After a seizure, the vet will give your dog a thorough examination, including a full neurological check, and will probably recommend blood tests. Normal results often lead to a diagnosis of idiopathic epilepsy (that is, of no known cause) but cannot rule out brain tumor, for which an MRI scan would be needed.

For an intact female who is having seizures, neutering will be advised by the vet. There are various drug options for treating epilepsy, although the vet may not start treatment after just one incident. Side effects can include drowsiness and weight gain. Regular monitoring is needed to ensure that the drug is at the correct level in the blood to control seizures without causing adverse effects. Over time, the dosage may have to be increased or other drugs added. To treat status epilepticus, the dog is kept under a general anesthetic until the vet allows recovery of consciousness in the hope that seizures will not resume.

> **"After a seizure** your dog may **rapidly return** to **normal**, but he could be **distant** and **disoriented** for a few hours."

◁ **TV trigger**
The flickering light of a television screen is sometimes found to be the cause of a dog having a seizure, but more commonly the triggers of seizures are not so obvious.

Inherited seizures
Epilepsy is inherited in several breeds, including Beagles. The first incident usually occurs in young dogs aged between six months and three years old.

Traffic accidents

Take every precaution to protect your dog from traffic accidents and prevent him from endangering other road users. Always keep him on a lead when walking on or near a road, however well trained he may be.

Emergency aid

If a dog is injured in a traffic accident, call your veterinarian for advice. Also contact the police if the accident happened on a public roadway. Legally, the driver of the vehicle that hit the dog must stop and give his or her details to the person in charge of the dog. If the dog is on its own then the driver must report the incident to the police within 24 hours. The dog may have open wounds, internal injuries, fractures, or a combination of injuries. Move him only if you feel it will not cause further injury, or if there is a danger of the dog being hit by another vehicle. Above all, take care not to endanger yourself. Using a blanket as a stretcher between two people is ideal.

Carefully maneuver the dog onto it while bearing in mind that a dog in pain may snap without warning and without meaning to do so. If you are on your own, and the casualty is not a big dog, then it may be a matter of having to scoop him up in your arms to remove him out of the path of traffic.

If you can transport the injured dog to a vet practice yourself,

> "**Move** a dog **only** if it will not cause **further injury.** Take **care** not to **endanger yourself**."

▽ **Waiting for help**
An injured dog may be unconscious or conscious and will probably be in shock and in pain. Keep him warm until help comes. Make sure that you do not put yourself at risk while tending to him.

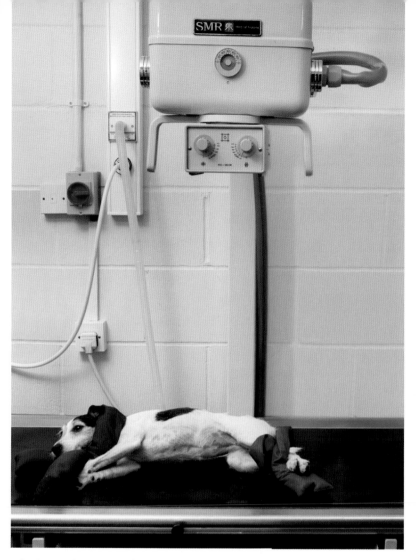

◁ **Positioned for radiology**
The vet may use images from an X-ray machine to examine an injured dog, in case there is hidden damage to internal organs such as the liver, kidneys, and bladder.

Minimizing the risks

■ Keep your dog on a short lead when walking along the side of any road or lane.

■ Keep fence gates closed and boundaries secure so your dog cannot escape.

■ Make sure your dog is obedient and responds immediately to your commands of stay and sit.

telephone ahead to advise that you are on your way. Otherwise, keep the animal warm while waiting for help to arrive. A survival blanket would be ideal if available, but improvising with anything such as a warm coat or sweater will still improve the dog's chances of survival. If there is heavy bleeding, apply pressure with some fabric.

If the injured dog is not with his owner, look for identification. He should have a disc on his collar engraved with contact details for his owner. Failing that, his breed, color, sex, and approximate age will help with identification later. If a microchip is found when he is scanned, then contacting the owner should be straightforward, provided the owner has kept his registration information up to date.

Treatment

Once at the veterinary practice, the priorities will be to provide pain relief, treat the dog for shock with intravenous fluids, and establish the extent of the injuries. Knowledge of preexisting conditions and medications will be invaluable but only likely if the dog has been identified and there is full access to his medical history.

Before giving treatment, the vet will do blood tests to gather information about the dog's general health and to look for signs of internal injuries. X-rays of the chest and abdomen, coupled with ultrasound scanning, will help to identify internal bleeding and organ damage. Fractures may be suspected from a physical examination of the dog, and can be confirmed with X-rays of the appropriate areas.

Except in the case of life-threatening problems that call for immediate surgery, such as a major hemorrhage, an operation requiring general anesthetic will be postponed until the dog's condition is stable.

Choking and poisoning

It is in a dog's nature to chew or eat anything that looks promising, but it is a habit that can get him into serious trouble. If your dog chokes on something or swallows a poisonous substance, you need to act quickly.

Choking

A dog can choke on all manner of objects, including bones, rawhide chews, wood, or children's toys. He may paw frantically at his mouth if the object is wedged between his teeth or across the roof of his mouth, and he may have difficulty breathing if the object is obstructing his airway. He may also drool profusely.

Only attempt to retrieve the object from your dog's mouth if you will not be bitten or there is no risk of pushing it further into the throat. Putting something across your dog's jaw to prevent him from closing his mouth is a good idea if it does not make it harder to retrieve the object. Ideally, use something rubbery or a pad of material to avoid damaging his teeth; never use a muzzle.

If you cannot remove the object, or are concerned that your dog's mouth has been damaged, then reassure him and take him straight to a vet. Telephone first to tell them there is an emergency.

If you see your dog swallow something he should not, such as a small piece of jewelry, a button, or a stone, contact your vet for advice. Very small objects may pass through your dog without causing a problem. A larger item may cause a blockage and need to be removed, preferably from the stomach through an endoscope before it has entered the intestines.

Poisoning

The most common way for a dog to be poisoned is by scavenging through things not intended for him. If you are worried that your dog may have eaten forbidden foods or substances, or he has persistent vomiting or diarrhea,

▽ **Dangerous bones**
A bone can pose a choking hazard if it is small enough to become wedged across the roof of the mouth or between the teeth, or if shards are swallowed and become stuck in the gullet.

▷ **Algae risk**
Some species of blue-green algae found in both fresh and salt water can cause fatal poisoning. If your dog loves a dip, try to find out if there is any record of contaminated water in your area.

▽ **Raiding the trash**
A dog's dietary indiscretions include raiding the trash can. Use containers such as step-on or mechanical push opening cans, which will not yield to a dog's inquisitive nose.

contact your veterinary practice right away for advice, because taking early action can be lifesaving. Keep any packaging to show the vet.

The home is potentially a very dangerous place (pp.24–5). It is extraordinary just what a dog will eat, given the chance. Take preventive action by always storing anything remotely edible out of reach. This includes all medication, both veterinary and human; antifreeze (ethylene glycol), which has a sweet taste but will cause kidney failure if drunk by a dog; weed killers and slug bait, which are easily picked up in the garden; and household cleaners (even

if you keep them in an inaccessible cupboard, remember that your dog could also drink from a toilet that has a chemical released into the water whenever it is flushed).

Among foodstuffs, chocolate is highly appealing to a dog but is toxic if it has a high cocoa solid content. Onions and their relations, including leeks, garlic, and green onions, are also poisonous to dogs.

Generally, the smaller the dog, the smaller the amount of toxin needed to have an effect. However, this is not the case with grapes both fresh and dried (raisins and currants), which are recognized as potential poisons. A small dog may eat a bunch of grapes and have no

problems, while a large dog may eat only a few and be very ill. The dried grapes, ingredients in many baked goods such as cakes, are by far the most toxic, and eating them can lead to serious problems such as kidney failure and pancreatitis.

Rat poison

Bait to control rodents should be used and stored well out of your dog's reach. Commonly available rat poisons interfere with the action of vitamin K, which is essential to the body's normal blood clotting process. This causes internal bleeding, which will not become immediately apparent. If you know or suspect that your dog has eaten rat poison, or a poisoned rodent, contact your vet and take the dog straight to the office, together with any relevant packaging.

"The home is potentially a very dangerous place. Store anything edible out of reach."

Bites and stings

Dogs are naturally inquisitive, exploring with their noses, so bites and stings from venomous animals or insects tend to be on the head and legs. Identifying the culprit will ensure your dog receives the right treatment.

Snakes

Venomous snakes are encountered in various natural environments worldwide. Their toxicity depends on the species, the amount of venom injected relative to the size of the dog, and the site of the bite.

The effects of a snake bite develop rapidly, within two hours. The puncture wounds from the bite are often visible, with painful swelling developing. A bitten dog may become lethargic and show other signs of poisoning, including overheating, rapid heart rate and panting, pale mucous membranes, excessive salivation, and vomiting. In severe cases, the liver, kidneys, and blood-clotting system may be affected, and the dog may go into shock or a coma.

Do not attempt to suck out the venom or apply a tourniquet. Speed is of the essence, so contact a veterinary practice and go there without delay. If a specific antivenom is to be used in the treatment of your dog, you need to be able to identify what bit him. If you are not certain of the species you could take photographs of the culprit, provided this is possible without endangering yourself.

Bees and wasps

These are a common risk to dogs both indoors and outdoors. If your dog is stung, move him quickly to avoid further stings and to avoid being stung yourself. Carefully check for insects trapped in your dog's coat and look for the site of the sting. Bees leave their stinger behind, so remove it carefully with tweezers if you can do this without squeezing the poison sac. Wasps can sting repeatedly, although they may leave the stinger in the skin. Bathe the area with baking soda dissolved in water (for bee stings) or with vinegar (for wasp stings), then apply antihistamine cream. Distract your dog or cover the area to prevent him from licking at it.

If your dog is in pain or his condition deteriorates, take him to the vet. Some dogs develop hives or multiple bumps under the skin. It is an emergency situation if your dog has been stung in the mouth or develops a severe allergic reaction.

Toads

When a toad feels threatened, it releases venom from its skin glands, which may be taken into a dog's mouth if he licks the toad or

Anaphylactic shock

Occasionally, a dog may have an extreme reaction shortly after exposure to something to which he is acutely sensitive—for example, bee venom, especially if he has had multiple stings. This severe allergic reaction, which is known as anaphylactic shock, can be a life-threatening situation. Initial signs of anaphylactic shock include vomiting and excitability, rapidly leading on to breathing difficulties, collapse, coma, and death. Emergency treatment is needed at a veterinary practice if the dog is to survive.

picks it up. A dog will react to toad venom with excessive salivation and may froth at the mouth and become very anxious. Carefully flush out his mouth with water and seek advice from your vet if you are concerned. The toxicity of toad venom varies between species. Exposure to the venom of the cane toad, *Bufo marinus,* is a serious situation. Flush out the dog's mouth and take him to a veterinary practice for emergency attention.

Creatures to avoid
A chance encounter with something that bites or stings can be painful and frightening for your dog.

Rattlesnake

Bee

Cane toad

> **"**It is an **emergency situation** if your dog has been **stung and** develops an **allergic reaction."**

Lurking in the undergrowth
Poisonous snakes, stinging insects, and other dangers can remain hidden in long grass until disturbed by an exploring nose. If your dog is bitten or stung, attend to him quickly and keep him calm.

Heat stroke and hypothermia

The effects of either overheating or exposure to cold can be fatal to a dog. Yet, with a little care and forethought, such a disaster is nearly always avoidable. Old or sick dogs and puppies are especially susceptible.

Heat stroke

If a dog overheats, he cannot cool down again by sweating as humans do. In such situations such as being confined in a car on a hot day or shut in a screened porch at home, especially if there is no drinking water available, your dog can rapidly develop heat stroke. This is a dangerous condition in which the body's temperature-regulating mechanism breaks down. The trend of dressing up dogs in canine clothing has also been responsible for some cases of overheating, particularly when owners have neglected to undress their dogs when indoors.

Heat stroke is a real medical emergency: without urgent veterinary attention, a dog can die from overheating within as little as 20 minutes. Signs include panting, distress, and reddening of the gums, with rapid progression to collapse, coma, and ultimately death. The priority is to remove the dog from the hot place to somewhere cool or take off his unwanted clothing. If a delay in taking him to a veterinary clinic is unavoidable, then you should cover him with wet sheets or towels, which can be kept over him while he is transported. Alternatively, put the dog in a bath of cold water or run a steady stream of water over him from a garden hose. Ice packs or bags of frozen vegetables can be used, and a fan will also help to cool him down.

Heat stroke is easily avoided simply by not leaving your dog in the car. It really is not enough just to leave the windows open, even if you have parked in the shade.

The situation is particularly risky if there are several dogs in the car, or your dog is already hot and panting from recent exercise.

Hypothermia

The reverse of heat stroke is hypothermia, when the body's core temperature falls to dangerously low levels. This is another emergency that is easily avoided. In cold weather, your dog can develop hypothermia if he is kept outside in a drafty kennel, or left in an unheated room or a car. Going into a pond or lake in winter can also lead to hypothermia. Puppies and old dogs are the most vulnerable.

A dog with hypothermia may shiver or move stiffly and appear lethargic. He needs warming up gradually out of the cold and kept covered with a blanket until he can be taken to a vet. A hypothermic dog will be given sterile warm fluids directly into a vein to help restore his core body temperature, together with treatment for shock.

> **"Heat stroke** is a real **medical emergency:** without **urgent attention** a dog can **die** in **20 minutes."**

◁ **Living outside**
A kennel protects your dog from wind and rain, but temperatures inside may soar in the summer, and plummet in the winter unless you can provide safe heating.

Danger of overheating
Despite the window being down, a car quickly becomes an oven, even at only moderately warm temperatures. Left shut in, this dog would be at risk of heat stroke.

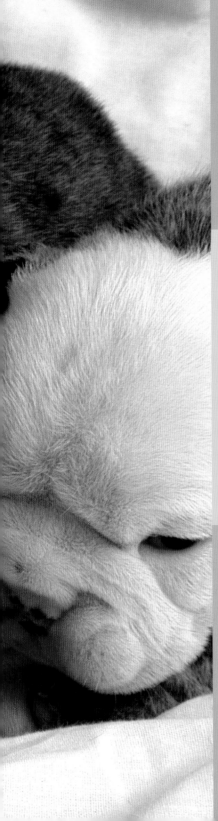

6

Breeding

Responsible breeding

Making the decision to breed from your dog should not be taken lightly. Not only is it an expensive and time-consuming process, but it can result in adding to the enormous surplus of dogs without homes.

Consider the reasons

Before you breed from your dog, it is important to think long and hard about your reasons for wanting to have a litter of puppies. Never breed to make money (remember that once you have paid stud fees, equipment costs, and food and vet bills there is little money to be made). It is easy to get carried away with thoughts of cute puppies playing around your home, but the reality is that rearing a litter is extremely hard work. They require daily care and attention as they grow. It may be that your dog has such a lovely temperament or good looks that you feel that it is your duty to create puppies with similar qualities. Unfortunately, it is rarely that simple due to the way traits are inherited, and there is no guarantee that the next generation will be the same as the last.

If you are considering breeding because you want another dog yourself, instead spare one of the hundreds of thousands of dogs in rescue homes and shelters. There are many benefits from adopting an older dog (pp.18–9). Often they may already be house-trained and socialized and any personality traits or problem behaviors are already evident. This makes it easier to pick a dog that suits your temperament and lifestyle.

If you have your heart set on a puppy, it is best to find a reputable professional breeder who can also give you the reassurance of their years of experience.

> "**Before** you **breed** your dog, **think long and hard—never breed** to **make money.**"

Non-pedigree pregnancies

If you do not intend to breed your female, it is advisable to have her neutered. However, occasionally accidents happen and unplanned matings occur. Speak to your vet immediately to discuss your options since it may be that stopping the pregnancy is advisable for the health of your dog. It could also be that the other dog is unknown to you or he has no pedigree, in which case you should speak to your vet about the best ways to re-home the puppies after they are born.

◁ **Handling new lives**
Puppies are an adorable addition to any household, but they require a huge investment of time and effort. The first few weeks will determine a puppy's character for life so you need to give them full-time care and attention.

△ **Pedigree pair**
When choosing the perfect breeding partner,
make sure you know the ancestry of both dogs;
it helps to determine how closely related they
are to prevent inbreeding.

▷ **Mating call**
In heat females release a powerful scent to
advertise their desire to mate. If your female is
in heat and not neutered yet, she may become
pregnant if allowed to wander.

If you are still set on having pups
from your current dog, first ask
yourself the following questions:
- Can you find homes for all
the puppies?
- Do you have the knowledge to
advise these potential owners,
some of whom may never have
owned a dog before?
- Do you have the flexibility to
spend weeks at home looking after
the puppies once they are born?
- Do you have adequate space, not
just for the litter to be born but for
a litter of six-week-old puppies?
  If you have considered everything
and are still certain breeding from
your dog is the right decision, do
lots of research and plan
everything carefully.

The perfect partner

Deciding which dog to mate with
yours is a difficult decision. Always
consult with a breed specialist to
discuss possible inherited diseases
and disorders such as hip dysplasia,
blindness, and deafness (pp.104–5).
You may also want to carry out
screening tests that will help detect
any potential conditions and
eliminate the likelihood of these
diseases occurring. Analyze where
your dog has weaknesses and
choose a mate that can improve
upon those areas. Research the
pedigree of both dogs to spot
potential problems. Remember
even an ideal screening result will
not guarantee that your puppy
won't develop a chronic disorder.

When you have chosen the male
dog, always meet him to make sure
his temperament is desirable.
Figure out when your female will
come into heat—it may vary from
breed to breed—and contact the
male dog's owner to arrange when
and where the dogs will meet.
Monitor the mating process, but
ideally do not interfere too closely.
Time will tell if your female is
pregnant, and you need to look
out for the signs (pp.172–3).

Pregnancy and prenatal care

Dogs are pregnant for 63 days but be prepared for puppies to arrive a few days on either side of this since the exact date depends on when actual fertilization occurred. During this time your dog will need extra care.

Early signs

Let your vet know early on that you have had your female mated; the vet will be an invaluable source of advice throughout your dog's pregnancy. Only your vet will be able to accurately diagnose whether your dog is pregnant during the early stages. If you can wait, you should be able to see for certain about five weeks into the pregnancy. Indicators that a dog is pregnant include a darkening and enlarging of the teats, light vaginal discharge, and abdominal swelling. If your dog has already had previous litters, her breast development may begin only in her last week of pregnancy. If she is carrying only one or two pups, or is plump anyway, the pregnancy may be difficult to spot. Some dogs appear to "drop" overnight as they suddenly change body shape.

Other changes to look out for are nausea and increased urination. It is also very common for dogs to undergo changes in their coat, with many dogs looking particularly glossy during pregnancy. Your dog may also display unusual

> **"Only your vet** will be able to **accurately diagnose** whether your dog is **pregnant** during the **early stages."**

△ **Digging behavior**
Dogs will often show an urge to dig that may increase as they near the end of their pregnancy; this is a natural instinct.

behaviors, such as digging or scratching. These are perfectly normal since your dog is planning where she is going to have her litter and she should not be punished. Make sure she has an outlet for this urge such as newspapers indoors or a grassy area in the yard.

Care during pregnancy

It is important to take extra measures to keep your dog parasite-free to ensure that she doesn't inadvertently pass any infestations on to her puppies. Your vet will be able to advise you on the best method of treatment for pregnant dogs. There is no need to increase the amount of food your dog eats in the early stages of pregnancy. However, at around six

weeks the food needs to be increased by about 10 percent each week. At this time your dog's exercise requirements are also likely to change. Shorter, more frequent walks that avoid very energetic activities are best. Particularly as she nears the end of her pregnancy, your dog may be reluctant to go far from home, though she will still need frequent trips outside to relieve herself.

Preparation for whelping

Long before your dog is due to have her puppies, set up a whelping area. The location of this is vital.

△ Food requirements
There should be no need to supplement your pregnant dog's food with additional vitamins as long as the food is of a high quality, but you will need to gradually increase the quantities.

It should be in the house so that your dog feels comfortable and the puppies get used to everyday household noises. However, it also needs to be out of the way in a place where few people will need to walk through once the puppies are born. It should be warm, dry, quiet, and draft-free. Spend time getting your dog used to going into her whelping area, particularly if it is in an area of the house she wouldn't normally go.

The whelping box itself can be either store-bought or homemade. Speak to a reputable breeder to get tips on the best design for your dog. A breeder may also be able to loan you one of his whelping boxes, but extreme care needs to be taken to prevent cross-contamination. The best whelping boxes are walled all the way around with a single gap to allow the dog access. The gap needs to have a lip that is high enough to prevent the puppies from wriggling out onto the floor but low enough to allow the mother to step over easily, even when in the late stages of pregnancy. The base of the whelping box must be lined with newspaper, which can be easily replaced. To keep the puppies warm, use a heat source such as a heat lamp but fix it high enough to prevent the mother from accidentally burning herself.

▽ Whelping area
Spend time making sure that your dog feels relaxed in the whelping area and get her used to you going in with her. Keep her favorite toys or blanket in the box to make it more inviting.

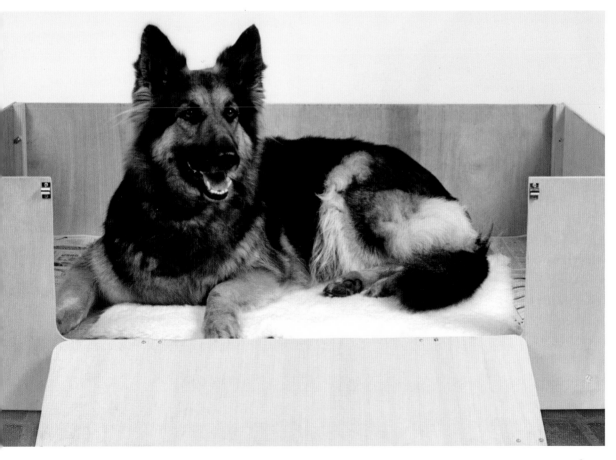

Whelping

Whelping can be a daunting prospect, however it normally occurs without any problems. The key to a smooth whelping is preparation so that you know what to expect and what to do if things start going wrong.

Whelping checklist

- A flashlight to keep a close eye on your dog should she need to go to the bathroom.
- Clean towels.
- Spare newspapers and trash bags.
- Thermometer.
- Notebook and pen to monitor temperature changes.
- Disinfectant.
- Latex gloves.
- A box containing a hot water bottle covered in a towel.
- Phone and vet's number.

Signs of whelping

As you approach your dog's delivery date, it becomes vital to keep a close eye on her. Individual dogs vary drastically in their behavior but there are some telltale signs which you should look out for to alert you to the fact that whelping is imminent.

Approximately 24 hours before your dog starts whelping, she is likely to become restless because of the discomfort she will feel as her body prepares to expel the puppies. At this stage your dog is also likely to refuse food. This is not something to worry about since she will more than make up for her lack of appetite once she has delivered all of her puppies. You may well notice your dog begin to pant very deeply and also start to scratch and dig at the bedding of the whelping box. This behavior originates from an instinctive desire to build a nest and should be encouraged by providing newspaper for her to rip up.

One of the most reliable indications that whelping will occur within the next 24 hours is a drop in body temperature of about 34°F (1°C). For this reason, getting your dog used to having her temperature taken on a daily basis is good planning throughout her

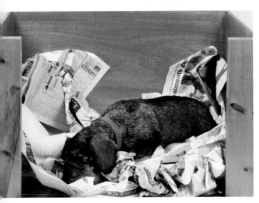

△ **Pre-labor signs**
Provide plenty of newspaper in the whelping box, which your dog can shred leading up to the start of whelping. She may move in circles before lying down. This behavior can continue for up to 12 hours before she gives birth.

▷ **Giving birth**
After giving birth, your dog will strip off the membrane of the amniotic sac and sever the umbilical cord with her teeth. You should only intervene if she appears to be biting the cord too closely or pulling too vigorously.

> "Your dog will be **visibly calm** just before **the arrival** of the **first puppy**."

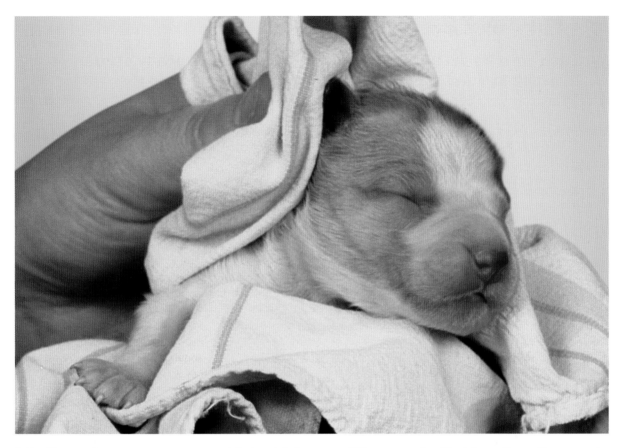

△ Handling a newborn puppy
Take a moment to check each puppy over and rub them dry with a clean towel. Then return the pup to the mother without delay.

pregnancy. Immediately prior to whelping beginning, strings of mucus will appear from the dog's vulva as the cervical plug that has protected the developing puppies from infection disintegrates.

The whelping process

Your dog will be visibly calm just before the arrival of the first puppy, and you should be able to see the muscles around her abdomen contract as she makes efforts to push the first puppy out. Initially you will probably only be able to see the black, fluid-filled amniotic sac, containing the puppy, appear at the vulva. Allow the dog to stand or lie down as she prefers, but be

ready to catch the puppy if it looks like it is going to drop some distance to the floor or over the side of the whelping box. If you see the puppy born with its rear end or back feet first, don't be alarmed because this is quite usual.

Normally your dog will remove the amniotic sac instinctively and begin licking the puppy to stimulate breathing. Ideally she should be left to do this herself; it is only advisable to intervene if she appears to be ignoring the puppy completely. Do not be alarmed if she starts nibbling at the puppy's stomach—she is simply severing the umbilical cord and should be allowed to do so. Once the puppy has been born, the placenta associated with that puppy should follow. This is a good source of energy and nutrients and poses no

health risks, so the mother can eat it if she chooses. However, it is important that you count the placentas as they are passed to ensure none have been retained once whelping has finished.

The period of time to wait until the next puppy is passed can vary greatly. During that time, the puppies that have already been born should be encouraged to suckle and your dog urged to tend to them. Take care that she does not inadvertently step on any of the puppies when giving birth to the next. If she becomes agitated, remove the puppies to a box containing a towel-covered hot-water bottle until the next puppy is born. When some time has passed, and your dog appears relaxed and attentive to her pups, the whelping process is over.

Postnatal care

With the worries of the whelping process now behind you, all your focus must switch to making sure that your dog has everything that she needs and that her puppies get the best possible start in life.

Care of the mother

The natural maternal instincts your dog has toward her puppies means that you will not need to do anything with the puppies initially. In fact, she will be so devoted to her puppies in the early days that you will find it difficult to persuade her to leave them even to go to the bathroom. She certainly won't need any exercise and she will only need to be taken out for short visits to relieve herself a few times a day.

Allow your dog to do what comes naturally to her. She should periodically lick the puppies to stimulate them to pass urine and feces, which she will consume. This process, combined with the placentas eaten during whelping, may cause your dog to have diarrhea, resulting in fluid loss. As a result she will require a lot of water. Her food intake will also need to increase because lactation requires a huge amount of energy. It is necessary to feed her about twice the number of calories she was consuming prior to whelping, and the meals need to be little and often. Since she will be reluctant to leave her puppies, feeding her in the whelping box is advisable.

Care of the puppies

The puppies themselves should not be interfered with, other than to be checked over to ensure they are healthy and are putting on weight. Although born with their eyes and ears closed, puppies have a good sense of smell and will naturally navigate themselves to the teats, with gentle nudges from their mother. Your dog's first milk (called colostrum) is vital to the puppies' health, and you need to be observant for any puppy that does not seem to be getting as much access to milk as the others. This means you will need to identify puppies early, either by body markings or by placing different colored yarn or collars on each one. Be careful though since puppies grow startlingly fast and will need their collars loosened regularly.

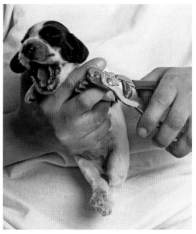

△ **Nail trimming**
Within a couple of weeks you will need to trim the puppies' nails to keep them from causing damage to their mother as they suckle.

◁ **Suckling**
The puppies get essential antibodies from their mother's first milk, which protects them against diseases. Growing pups will still need to suckle until they are about eight weeks old.

▷ **Keeping puppies clean**
Licking is a hugely important activity for the health of the puppies. It cleans and stimulates the puppies and also encourages bonding between the mother and her youngsters.

Be alert for any signs of a problem developing in any of the puppies, particularly in the first 36 hours after whelping. A healthy puppy is warm and dry to the touch with an elastic quality to his skin. Fading Puppy Syndrome, where puppies get progressively weaker soon after whelping, often results in the puppy dying. It may be kinder to call for your vet to humanely euthanize the pup to prevent prolonged suffering. Healthy puppies are constantly moving and twitching, so if any of them are totally still or are making noise incessantly, call a vet immediately.

Tips on bottle feeding

■ Only bottle feed puppies as a last resort.

■ Buy a special pet feeding bottle or premature baby bottle from a pet shop or your vet.

■ Stimulate the puppy to go to the bathroom before feeding.

■ Use a formula with a high protein and fat content. Ask your vet if you are not sure which brand to use.

■ Sterilize all bottle-feeding equipment before each use.

Early puppy care

By the time the puppies are a few weeks old, you will constantly have them at your feet, and their care becomes a full-time job. This is the most important time of the pups' lives and there is much to prepare them for.

The first few weeks

The puppies will soon begin to develop teeth, at which point their diet should be supplemented with solid food as well as plenty of chew toys to help the teething process. Introduce solid food slowly and in tiny quantities at first so that the puppies get used to digesting it. Make sure you buy specially formulated puppy food, which is high in energy with the correct balance of nutrients (p.42). Your dog will need some time away from the puppies as her feeding responsibilities dwindle. This will also speed up the weaning process, getting the puppies used to being away from their mother. Up until now your dog will have kept the puppies clean, so expect much more mess as you begin weaning the puppies. Use a warm damp cloth to clean their faces and fur.

Newborn development

All puppies develop very quickly in their first two months of life. No matter what their size or breed, puppies go through the same stages during their development at roughly the same time.

◁ **One week**
Although born completely blind and deaf, puppies have a keen sense of smell and can easily locate their mother's teats to get food, warmth, and the comfort of snuggling up with the rest of the litter. During the first week they can't regulate their body temperature and will spend most of their time sleeping and suckling.

△ **Two weeks**
By the time a puppy is two weeks old, his eyes are starting to open but cannot focus properly. He is more active but is still unable to walk and will spend long periods sleeping.

△ **Three weeks**
By three weeks a puppy can see and hear well. He is gaining in strength rapidly and is starting to use his legs to support his body weight. He may even have started teething.

△ **Four weeks**
At this stage a puppy will start to play with his siblings, which further increases muscle strength. He will also become more vocal and growl during play. You may even hear an occasional bark.

△ **Six weeks**
Although still needing plenty of sleep, a six-week old puppy has all his milk teeth and is already eating solid food. He is excited to learn about his surroundings, which he does by exploring, sniffing, and chewing.

△ **Eight weeks**
Now independent of his mother's milk and with the necessary social skills for living in the company of others, an eight-week-old puppy is ready to leave his mother and siblings behind and start a new life as a member of a human family group. As a responsible breeder, you need to make sure that each puppy goes to a suitable, loving home that is well prepared to take care of all his needs.

◁ **Socializing**
Basic training is a fun and easy way to interact with young puppies who are extremely responsive and obedient. While introducing children, ask them to sit and offer small, tasty treats to the puppy. This will help him feel comfortable and approach people confidently.

▽ **House-training**
Get puppies habituated to using newspaper for going to the bathroom. Accidents will still happen but you will be easing the way for the new owners to finish the training.

Early training

As the puppies open their eyes and ears, they will become more mobile and inquisitive. At this stage it is important to include them in as many family activities as possible and help them socialize with people of all ages. Most puppies will go into a home environment and therefore, during these early weeks, getting them used to the sorts of sights and noises that accompany the daily comings and goings of a household is imperative.

The vast majority of dogs that end up in rescue shelters are those that are not adequately prepared for life outside the breeder's home. A lot of emphasis is put on the role of the new puppy owner, but by the time they collect the puppy from the breeder the main opportunity for early training and socialization has already passed. Teaching a few simple rules in the breeder's home can make the difference between a

> "Spending a **few minutes every day** with **each puppy** from your litter will allow you **to train** and **socialize them.**"

confident and well-adjusted puppy and one that is likely to develop behavioral problems.

It is entirely possible to train puppies before they go to their new homes so that they only relieve themselves on newspaper. This makes it much easier for the new owners to complete their house-training once they get their puppy home. In addition, spending a few minutes with each puppy every day will allow you to train them to do some basic behaviors on command, such as sit and lie down.

However, the most important factor of training is to socialize all your puppies with a range of everyday experiences such as

household noises, children playing, and overall handling and grooming. This responsibility falls to you as the breeder, so when they are only a few weeks old, puppies will happily accept new experiences with minimal reassurance.

At around 10 weeks old, puppies become significantly less inquisitive and more wary of any novel experiences. This fear is a natural protection as they stray further from the den and into danger, but makes the job of a new puppy owner potentially difficult. If a puppy has had good early socialization with the breeder, he will emerge from this wary stage a confident youngster.

Finding new homes

Having invested so much time in the planning and rearing of your dog's puppies, you will naturally be very attached to them. Your next responsibility is to ensure that you send them to the best possible homes.

Advertising

You are likely to want to advertise your puppies for sale locally, but also contact your country's breed societies and kennel club to place advertisements. Thoughtful advertising will help ensure you get the right people inquiring. For example, consider placing an ad with your veterinarian as opposed to the local newspaper. Likewise, avoid free ads or online websites that could attract inappropriate interest. Always remember that your safety and that of your puppies is paramount, so be careful when inviting unknown people into your home.

Encourage prospective owners to visit often and give them as much information as possible to prepare them. You should also inform them about inherited disorders and general care and training. It is always a good idea to refer the new owners to breed societies and ask them to join so they have a good support network throughout their dog's life. Finally, make it clear that they have the option to return the puppy to you if they can no longer look after him. Your support of new owners in these first weeks can build a lasting bond that will mean you stay in contact and get frequent updates of your puppies.

182

Breeding

Questions to ask potential owners:

- Why do you want a dog?
- Where do you live?
- Have you owned dogs before? And do you have prior experience of this breed?
- How much time can you spend at home with the dog?
- Who will care for the dog in your absence?
- Do you lead an active lifestyle?
- Do you have other pets?
- Do you have a baby, children, or elderly relatives at home?

> **"Your support of new owners** in these first weeks can **build** a **lasting friendship."**

Assessing new owners

Spend time getting to know each puppy's future owner so that you can start preparing your puppy for the lifestyle he is going to become a part of. If your pup is going to a family with young children, it is vital to get him used to them. If you do not have young children of your own, you may need to invite over those of friends or neighbors.

▷ **Meeting prospective owners**
The way potential owners interact with a puppy can tell you a lot about them. Never be afraid to refuse to sell a puppy to anyone if you don't think they will provide a suitable home.

Lasting friendship
Take extra care when introducing children and puppies. Make sure that the child understands how to interact with their new puppy correctly and train the pup to behave appropriately around children too.

Glossary

Glossary

ANESTHETIC
A drug used to stop a dog from feeling pain during an operation. A general anesthetic, usually given as a gas or injection, renders a dog temporarily unconscious. A local anesthetic numbs a small area of the body.

ANTIEMETIC
A medicine used to stop vomiting.

ANTIHISTAMINE
A medicine used to relieve the symptoms of allergy, such as itching or sneezing.

BREED
A group of dogs that share specific aspects of appearance and behavior passed on from one generation to the next.

CORTICOSTEROID
A drug used to relieve inflammation, joint pain, or allergic symptoms such as itching.

CROSSBREED
A dog produced from parents of different breeds. Differs from a "mixed-breed" dog (also sometimes called a mongrel), whose parents are of no particular breed.

DOUBLE COAT
A coat comprising two layers of hair: a dense, warm undercoat, and a longer, weather-resistant topcoat.

ECG
Short for "electrocardiography," a diagnostic test in which an instrument is used to record the electrical activity in the heart. ECG is used to detect problems such as an abnormal heart rhythm.

ELIZABETHAN COLLAR
A large, cone-shaped plastic collar that is fitted around a dog's neck and head, facing forward. It is designed to stop a dog from licking or biting wounds on its body, and is used to protect an injured area or surgical incision.

ENDOSCOPE
A viewing instrument including a rigid or flexible tube, often with a light and a camera at the tip, which is used to look inside body passages such as the esophagus (gullet).

HABITUATION
The process of getting a dog used to a stimulus (a source of stress or excitement, such as a noisy household appliance) by gradually exposing the dog to that stimulus until he no longer reacts to it.

HAND SIGNAL
A distinct gesture used to give a dog a specific command.

HAND-STRIPPING
A grooming technique in which dead hair is pulled out of a dog's coat either by hand or with a stripping knife; used on non-molting breeds with a wiry topcoat.

HEELING
Training your dog to walk close by your side, either on or off the lead.

HOUSE-TRAINING
Training a puppy or dog to relieve himself outdoors rather than in the home.

HYPOALLERGENIC DIET
A restricted diet used to identify and control food allergies. Some pet food manufacturers produce special hypoallergenic foods for dogs.

MRI
Short for "magnetic resonance imaging," a medical scanning technique in which magnetic fields and radio waves are used to produce an image of internal body tissues.

MUZZLE
A device made of cloth, leather, or plastic, used to stop a dog from biting. It fits over a dog's nose and mouth and is fastened at the back of the head.

NEUTERING
The removal of a dog's reproductive organs so it cannot produce puppies. In males it involves castration (removal of the testicles), and in females it involves spaying (removal of the uterus and ovaries). Non-neutered males and females are referred to as intact.

PEDIGREE
For a dog of a particular breed, the pedigree is a written record of that dog's recent ancestry. A pure-bred dog is sometimes referred to as a "pedigree" dog.

POSITIVE TRAINING
A style of training based on rewarding only desired behavior in a dog while ignoring unwanted behavior.

POSTNATAL
A term meaning "following birth": for example, postnatal care of a mother and her puppies.

PRENATAL
A term meaning "before birth": for example, prenatal care of a pregnant dog.

PUPPY TEETH
A dog's baby teeth, like those in a human child. Puppies lose their puppy teeth at about four to six months of age, as the adult teeth come through.

RAWHIDE
The tough inner layer of animal hides (such as cow, buffalo, or horse hide), used to make chewy toys and treats for dogs.

REWARD
A food treat or positive attention (such as vocal praise or strokes) given to a dog when he has done something correctly.

SELECTIVE BREEDING
Mating particular individuals of a certain breed in order to produce a desired characteristic or to eliminate undesired or unhealthy characteristics.

SLICKER BRUSH
A brush with a wide, flat head and thin metal bristles, designed to remove dead, matted hair.

SOCIALIZATION
The process of teaching your puppy to get used to new people and other animals.

TOPCOAT
The outer layer of a double coat, consisting of long, tough, weather-resistant hairs.

UNDERCOAT
The inner layer of a double coat, consisting of soft, warm, dense hairs.

VACCINATION
Also called immunization, a procedure used to prevent a dog from catching specific bacterial or viral infections. It involves inoculation—injecting a vaccine (a substance containing weakened or dead bacteria or viruses) into a dog. The dog's immune system attacks the organisms in the vaccine, and in so doing will "learn" to attack the actual disease organisms in the future.

VOICE CUE
A word or sound used when training a dog to do a specific action.

WEANING
The process by which puppies graduate from drinking their mother's milk to eating solid food. It naturally happens between three and six weeks of age.

WHELPING
For dogs, the term used for giving birth.

Useful contacts

US

SOURCES OF NEW DOGS AND PUPPIES

As well as breeders, reputable rescue organizations are a good source of new puppies and adult dogs. Try to find a center where they make the effort to assess all the dogs in their care so you can choose one to suit your temperament and lifestyle.

The following are useful organizations to contact when looking for a new dog:

American Society for the Prevention of Cruelty to Animals (ASPCA)
www.aspca.org
Tel: 212-876-7700
424 E. 92nd St,
New York, NY 10128-6804

The Humane Society of the United States
www.hsus.org
Tel: 202-452-1100
2100 L St, NW
Washington, DC 20037

For further information on breeders with puppies, contact:

American Kennel Club
www.akc.org
Tel: 919-233-9767
8051 Arco Corporate Drive, Suite 100,
Raleigh, NC 27617-3390

DOG AND PUPPY TRAINING

Dog and puppy training classes, or individual instruction, can help you to progress more rapidly and assist with any individual difficulties. Choose someone experienced and knowledgable, who uses only positive methods with both dogs and their owners. Other good sources of information about local trainers are local vets, groomers, and pet stores.

The following are useful organizations to contact when looking for a dog or puppy trainer:

Association of Pet Dog Trainers
www.apdt.com
Email: information@apdt.com
Tel: 800-738-3647
104 South Calhoun Street
Greenville, SC 29601

National Association of Dog Obedience Instructors
www.nadoi.org
Tel: 505-850-5957
PO Box 1439,
Socorro, NM 87801

BEHAVIOR PROBLEMS

If you are experiencing behavior problems with your dog, it is best to get help fast before habits become too established. Look for someone with both practical experience and academic knowledge. They should work on veterinary referral and be insured. Contact the following organizations or ask your vet to refer you to someone they trust:

The International Association of Animal Behavior Consultants
www.iaabc.org
Tel: 484-843-1091
565 Callery Road,
Cranberry Township, PA 16066

Animal Behavior Society
http://www.animalbehavior.org/

UK

SOURCES OF NEW DOGS AND PUPPIES

As well as breeders, reputable rescue organizations are a good source of new puppies and adult dogs. Try to find a center where they make the effort to assess all the dogs in their care so you can choose one to suit your temperament and lifestyle.

The following are useful organizations to contact when looking for a new dog:

Battersea Dogs and Cats Home
www.battersea.org.uk
Email: info@battersea.org.uk
Tel: 020 7622 3626
4 Battersea Park Road, London,
SW8 4AA

Dogs Trust
www.dogstrust.org.uk
Tel: 020 7837 0006
17 Wakley Street, London, EC1V 7RQ

Blue Cross
www.bluecross.org.uk
Tel: 0300 777 1897
Shilton Road, Burford, Oxon, OX18 4PF

Royal Society for the Prevention of Cruelty to Animals
www.rspca.org.uk
Tel: 0300 1234 555
RSPCA Enquiries Service, Wilberforce Way, Southwater, Horsham, West Sussex
RH13 9RS

For further information on breeders with puppies, contact:

The Kennel Club
www.thekennelclub.org.uk
Tel: 0844 463 3980
1-5 Clarges Street, Piccadilly, London,
W1J 8AB

DOG AND PUPPY TRAINING

Dog and puppy training classes, or individual instruction, can help you to progress more rapidly and assist with any individual difficulties. Choose someone experienced and knowledgable, who uses only positive methods with both dogs and their owners. Other good sources of information about local trainers are local vets, groomers, and pet stores.

The following are useful organizations to contact when looking for a dog or puppy trainer:

Association of Pet Dog Trainers
(national listings of pet dog trainers)
www.apdt.co.uk
Email: info@apdt.co.uk
Tel: 01285 810811
PO Box 17, Kempsford, GL7 4WZ

Puppy School
(UK network of puppy trainers)
www.puppyschool.co.uk
Email: info@puppyschool.co.uk
PO Box 186, Chipping Norton, OX7 3XG

BEHAVIOR PROBLEMS

If you are experiencing behavior problems with your dog, it is best to get help fast before habits become too established. Look for someone with both practical experience and academic knowledge. They should work on veterinary referral, and be insured. Contact the Association of Pet Behaviour Counsellors or ask your vet to refer you to someone they trust.

Association of Pet Behaviour Counsellors
www.apbc.org.uk
Email: info@apbc.org.uk
Tel: 01386 751151
PO Box 46, Worcester, WR8 9YS

Index

Index

191

Index

Acknowledgments

Dorling Kindersley would like to thank the following: Alice Bowden for proofreading and Helen Peters for the index. Supriya Mahajan, Swati Katyal, Gazal Roongta, and Vidit Vashisht for design assistance, and Nandini Gupta and Pallavi Singh for editorial assistance. Ben Bennett and John MacBrayne at Colne Valley Veterinary Practice, Colchester, and everyone who allowed their dogs to be photographed: Tina Brewers (Rio and Raffie), Rachel and Lilah Dixey (Dudley), Clare Hogston (Dottie), Alison and Anna Logan (Pippin and Smudge), John and Maureen Logan (Pippa), Angela Morgan (Ellie), Sandra Sibbons (Harry), and Kate Went. Candice and Polly at Posh Pet Parlour, Weybridge, for the grooming photography, and Tadley Pet Supplies for the loan of dog toys and equipment.

PICTURE CREDITS

The publisher would like to thank the following for their kind permission to reproduce their photographs:
l=left, r=right, t=top, c=center, a=above, b=below.

1 Getty Images: Hans Surfer / Flickr (c). **2-3 Alamy Images:** Juniors Bildarchiv GmbH. **4 Alamy Images:** Juniors Bildarchiv GmbH (bl). **Getty Images:** Daniel Grill (bc/Bulldog Puppy). **5 Dreamstime.com:** Alan Dyck (bc/Bulldog Puppies); Melinda Nagy (bl). **6 Getty Images:** Tetra Images (ca). **7 Getty Images:** Fry Design Ltd / Photographer's Choice (cra). **8 Fotolia:** pattie (cla). **9 FLPA:** Gerard Lacz (ca). **Getty Images:** Don Mason / Blend Images (cra). **10-11 Alamy Images:** Juniors Bildarchiv GmbH (l). **13 Dreamstime.com:** Michael Pettigrew (tc). **14 Getty Images:** Datacraft (cl). **16-17 Corbis:** Yoshihisa Fujita / MottoPet / amanaimages. **26 Dreamstime.com:** Hdconnelly (crb). **35 Fotolia:** Comugnero Silvana (cla). **Getty Images:** Boston Globe (tr). **36-37 Getty Images:** Daniel Grill (l). **37 Dreamstime.com:** Olena Adamenko (cb). **41 Alamy Images:** Juniors Bildarchiv GmbH. **42 Corbis:** Dale Spartas (cl). **Dreamstime.com:** Clearviewstock (br). **43 Dreamstime. com:** Ccat82 (cra). **Getty Images:** MIXA Co. Ltd. (tl). **44 Corbis:** Don Mason / Blend Images (clb). **46 Getty Images:** Tim Platt / Iconica (bl). **48-49 Alamy Images:** Juniors Bildarchiv GmbH. **50 Getty Images:** Tetra Images (ca). **51 Alamy Images:** Arco Images GmbH (cla). **Fotolia:** ctvvelve (ca). **54-55 Dreamstime.com:** Sixninepixels. **65 Alamy Images:** Juniors Bildarchiv GmbH (ca). **78 Alamy Images:** De Meester Johan / Arterra Picture Library (bl). **80 Getty Images:** Fry Design Ltd / Photographer's Choice (bl). **85 Corbis:** Konrad Wothe / Minden Pictures (br). **FLPA:** Erica Olsen (tl). **86-87 Getty Images:** Fotosearch. **88 Getty Images:** Jupiterimages / Brand X Pictures (bl); NBC / NBCUniversal (crb). **90 Corbis:** Stefan Wackerhagen / imagebroker (br). **Dreamstime.com:** Sally Wallis (clb). **91 Corbis:** Dale Spartas. **93 Corbis:** Alice Van Kempen / Foto Natura / Minden Pictures (ca). **102 Getty Images:** Anthony Brawley Photography / Flickr (cla). **105 Corbis:** Cheryl Ertelt / Visuals Unlimited (tl). **Getty Images:** Hans Surfer / Flicker (cra). **107 Dreamstime.com:** Roughcollie (br). **108-109 Alamy Images:** Juniors Bildarchiv GmbH. **110 Fotolia:** pattie (cb). **111 Alamy Images:** FLPA. **117 Alamy Images:** SuperStock (tr). **Dorling Kindersley:** Kim Bryan (tl). **118 Getty Images:** Christopher Furlong / Getty Images News (cra). **119 Dreamstime.com:** Dmitry Kalinovsky (bl). **123 Corbis:** Mark Raycroft / Minden Pictures (tr). **126 Alamy Images:** Juniors Bildarchiv GmbH (bl). **127 Dreamstime.com:** Yulia Chupina (br). **Getty Images:** Angela Wyant / Taxi (t). **128 Corbis:** Dale Spartas (br). **129 Corbis:** Alice Van Kempen / Foto Natura / Minden Pictures (t). **130 Corbis:** Yannick Tylle (bl). **131 Dreamstime.com:** Kitsen (tr); Liumangtiger (cla). **133 Fotolia:** Dogs (tr). **134 Alamy Images:** De Meester Johan / Arterra Picture Library (bl). **135 Alamy Images:** Realimage (t). **Science Photo Library:** Manfred Kage (clb). **136 Alamy Images:** Nigel Cattlin (bc). **137 Dreamstime.com:** Alice Herden. **138 Corbis:** Akira Uchiyama / Amanaimages (b). **139 Alamy Images:** Petra Wegner (tr). **Getty Images:** Lisa Vaughan / Flickr (tl). **140 Alamy Images:** Juniors Bildarchiv GmbH (b). **141 Dreamstime.com:** Valeriy Novikov (cra). **142 Getty Images:** Jeff J Mitchell / Getty Images News (br). **143 Alamy Images:** John Eccles (cr). **144-145 Corbis:** Dann Tardif / LWA. **150-151 Dreamstime.com:** Melinda Nagy (l). **152 Dreamstime.com:** Printmore (crb); Taviphoto (bl). **153 Fotolia:** Alexander Raths (tl). **154 Dreamstime.com:** Jolita Marcinkene (l). **156-157 Alamy Images:** Juniors Bildarchiv GmbH. **158 Alamy Images:** petographer (bc). **159 Corbis:** Marion Fichter / imagebroker. **165 Getty Images:** Back in the Pack dog portraits / Flickr. **167 Alamy Images:** Vicki Beaver. **168-169 Dreamstime.com:** Alan Dyck (l). **169 Corbis:** Jean-Christophe Bott / Epa (ca). **171 Alamy Images:** Tierfotoagentur (t). **173 Fotolia:** Dogs (tl). **175 FLPA:** Gerard Lacz (t). **177 Dreamstime.com:** Wenbin Yu (r). **178-179 Alamy Images:** Harry Page. **182 Getty Images:** Datacraft Co Ltd (br). **183 Getty Images:** Don Mason / Blend Images

All other images © Dorling Kindersley
For further information *see*:
www.dkimages.com